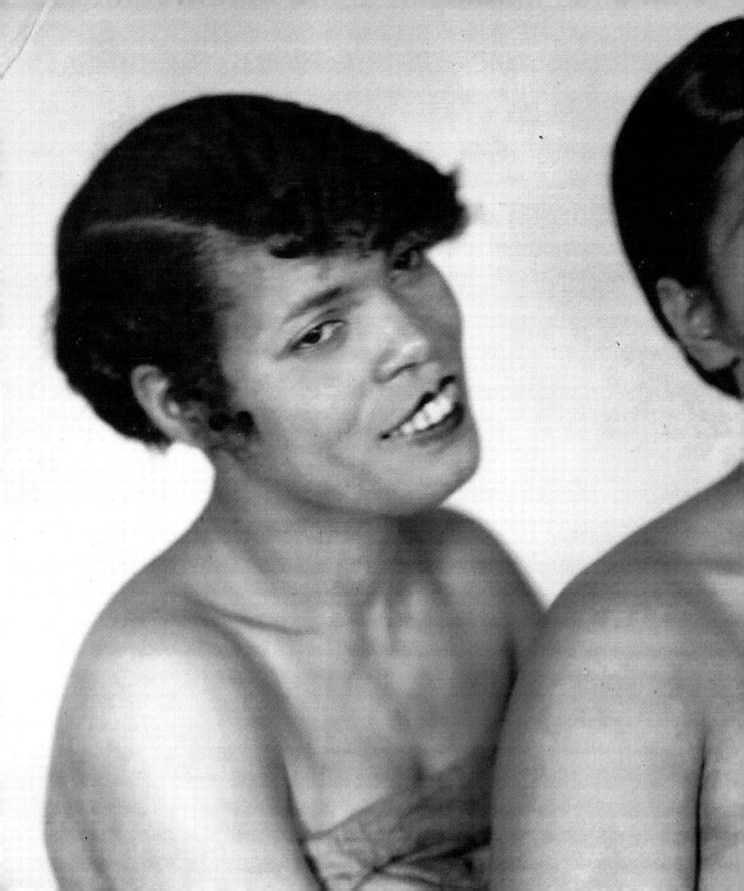

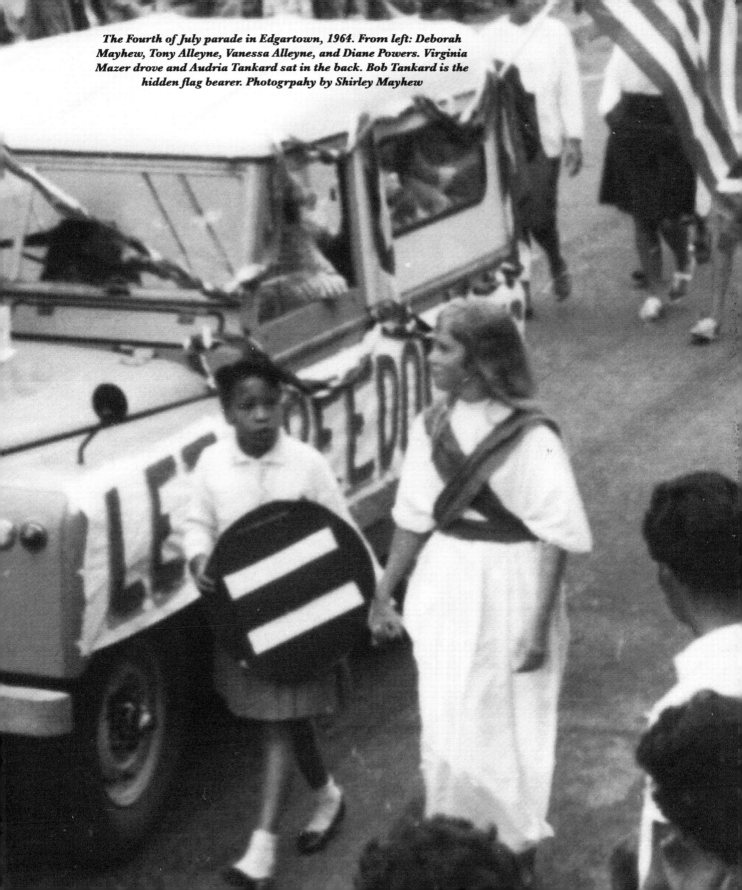

The Fourth of July parade in Edgartown, 1964. From left: Deborah Mayhew, Tony Alleyne, Vanessa Alleyne, and Diane Powers. Virginia Mazer drove and Audria Tankard sat in the back. Bob Tankard is the hidden flag bearer. Photogrpahy by Shirley Mayhew

The Heritage Trail gratefully acknowledges funding and support for this project received from the Massachusetts Foundation for the Humanities, Steve Bernier and Constance Messmer, Jeff and Susan Parker, Skip and Karen Finley, Tanya Lewis, Joseph and Rae Carter, Vera Shorter, Mickey Thompson and the Friends of the African American Heritage Trail. This project was enriched by Jaquelle Servance and Dana Carberry, models; Bronwyn Burns, Elyse Fortes, Lily Morris, Joe Murphy and Lauraye White, artists; John Belain, portrait artist; Erin Palacios and Carrie Camillo Tankard, essayists; Gaby Leon Guerrero and Sarah LaPiana, poets; Charlie Utz, Craig McCormack, Tony Bowyer and Mark Alan Lovewell, photographers; John Budris, editor; and Janet Holladay, book designer at the Tisbury Printer.

MASSACHUSETTS
FOUNDATION FOR THE
Humanities
Bringing Ideas to Life

TABLE OF CONTENTS

Good times and hard times,
they're all worth the telling.

The Martha's Vineyard African-American Heritage trail brings the local tribulations and triumphs of people of African heritage into public history. It acknowledges the presence of slavery in the first century and a half of English settlement; it showcases black men's participation in the whaling industry; it honors the efforts of Wampanoags and of white Vineyarders to protect persons threatened with the return to slavery by the Fugitive Slave Act; and it celebrates the Vineyard's vibrant black community of the 20th century. The chain of markers in all parts of the Island is an ornament that enhances the Vineyard.

—Frances Karttunen, author of The Other Islanders: People Who Pulled Nantucket's Oars.

REFLECTIONS ON BUILDING THE AFRICAN AMERICAN HERITAGE TRAIL

Elaine Cawley Weintraub

I'm for truth, no matter who tells it.
I'm for justice no matter who its for or against.

—Malcolm X

When I began this work many years ago it was in response to the need of the children I worked with. The quest began as a love letter to those children who had little to encourage them, but I would caution anyone who was about to "call out" injustice to prepare for some hard times. In the early days of this project, I was often surprised by the animosity shown to the development of the Trail. I received a great many academic recognitions, and the project thrived but I learned to acquire a thick skin and keep

Capt. and Sarah Martin's couch,
in the late Victorian Eastlake style.

my eyes firmly on the goal of creating the African American Heritage Trail. For every disappointment, there were many wonderful experiences and many unexpected allies.

The family of Doris Jackson and her daughter, Lee Van Allen, have been valued allies in the pursuit of this work and the various Town Boards who approved the placing of plaques on town land have supported the development of the Trail. The Land Bank organization on whose property two of the Heritage Trail sites are placed have been a resource for the project as have the Wampanoag Tribe of Aquinnah. Those whose family histories have been celebrated by our organization and whose stories have been saved for posterity have been unfailingly supportive.

As the work of the Trail has become well known it has been embraced by colleges, universities and numerous visitors to the Island in the summer. It has been an honor to share the stories previously uncelebrated and undocumented with both the academic community and the Island community.

One of the most significant developments of the African American Heritage Trail History Project has been the involvement of the history students at the Regional High School here on the Vineyard. It was a very important part of our mission to teach this history so that it will never again be lost. It is part of the Vineyard's history and the freshman students not only learn about the valuable contributions of people of color to the history of this Island, they research those stories adding more to what is known, and, most significantly, they grow up knowing that this is a diverse community with many stories all of value. Each year, the board of the African American Heritage Trail awards prizes for works of excellence.

The Trail organization has been inclusive and has honored people for their contributions to justice and equality regardless of their ethnicity. In the case of the dedication of St. Andrews church in Edgartown, our role was that of a peacemaker and consensus builder and the dedication of that site involved many sections of the Island community, and was emotionally and spiritually inspiring.

Some years ago, Dr. Tom Doyle, then owner of the Martin House on Chappaquiddick made a gift to me of an old couch that had belonged to William and Sarah Martin. It was basically just a frame, but it has now been reupholstered in a way that would look recognizable to the Martins. I often sit on it and reflect about where this project has gone from its humble beginnings in Oak Bluffs school, and the young children who inspired me. They are all grown up now, and life has not always been kind to them. They were the reason that this project began and because of them no other child will ever have to ask: "Where were all the black people then? Were they here?"

This has been a path made by walking, alliances have been made and unsung heroes celebrated. The Trail will continue to grow as the storytellers continue to reach out to us and the Trail itself is now a part of every town on the Island. This quest began as a search for lost heroes and we have found so many. The range of experiences that we celebrate is incredible and we give thanks for those whose lives were crowned with success and honor them, but we also remember those whose lives were hard working, unrecognized and ultimately, heroic.

Elaine Cawley Weintraub, 2015

Photo by Mark Alan Lovewell

"For the past several years, I have brought groups of teachers from communities in Massachusetts to tour the Martha's Vineyard African-American Heritage Trail and visit Dr. Elaine Cawley Weintraub's classroom to see how she integrates the Trail into the process of teaching United States history. As a result of these visits, many teachers have created heritage trails in their own communities

"The Trail is an effective way to present an inclusive history. It values the contributions and experiences of people of color and encourages students to do the same. Students come to realize that history is not just about kings and queens or governors and generals. They learn that we must consider the experiences of people from every strata of society in order to develop our a historical perspectives. Disenfranchised people did not leave their stories for us in journals. There was very little written of them in local newspapers. They do not appear in town genealogies. What Dr. Cawley Weintraub and her colleagues have done is bring their stories to life.

"This Trail has the potential to transform students' lives. It creates an awareness that can frame the way students view history and also current events. This Trail represents a new frontier in teaching history to our students, and it is certain to be replicated in other communities. By learning about how history influenced all residents in their local communities, students will develop their own balanced perspectives of state, national, and world history."

-Dr. Susan Dargan, Framingham State College

President Barack Obama plays basketball with White House staffers while on vacation on Martha's Vineyard, Aug. 26, 2009. Official White House Photo by Pete Souza

Barack Obama

We began this project many years ago seeking to find the lost heroes and undocumented achievements of the African-American community. A vital part of the mission has been to ensure that this important history will never again be lost or ignored. We were ambitious, but never did we imagine that in 2008 the first African-American president would be elected and that he would serve two terms. We are proud to say that President Barack Obama is a regular seasonal visitor to Martha's Vineyard, and that his presence here serves as an inspiration and a reminder of all that is possible.

The African-American Heritage Trail of Martha's Vineyard is a Community History Project dedicated to researching and documenting the previously unrecorded history of people of color on this Island. Our students act as teachers, archival researchers, graveyard landscapers, oral historians, and custodians of the sites. The Heritage Trail project is dedicated to the dissemination of the history of this Island to all our communities. Students are responsible for much of that role. Projects have been in concert with the Wampanoag Tribal Community and the Island towns. In addition, students continue to explore and write primary history through the study of the Trail at Martha's Vineyard Regional High School. We are proud to be affiliated with such an extraordinary history project.

—Margaret Regan, principal of Martha's Vineyard Regional High School

FOREWORD

Carrie Camillo Tankard

Little did I know when I left New Jersey after the Newark riots in 1967, that I would become involved in such a wonderful project as the African-American Heritage Trail of Martha's Vineyard. As I reflect on the Trail today, my mother's encouraging words come to mind: "You can do anything you want. Get involved in your surroundings."

She practiced what she preached. I remember how she put on her helmet for air raid drills during WW II and how she never missed a PTA meeting even as she grabbed up her purse and papers and ran out the door. So when the opportunity presented itself, I took her advice and jumped at the chance to help create something that would honor her and leave a legacy for my children and grandchildren.

History goes on and on, blending yesterday and today into tomorrow. Some ideas and values do not change. It is for that reason that the sites to the Landladies at Hiawatha

Park and South Circuit Avenue are my favorites on the Trail. In our research, we discovered so many women of color with great entrepreneurial skills. Considering the era in which these women lived, their accomplishments are even more impressive. The phrase " Women's Lib" had not even been coined yet. That term came many years later, but these strong African-American women had the foresight and courage to open businesses and guest houses so that other African-Americans could come to work, play and vacation here on Martha's Vineyard. These houses remain today and form an visible circle around Hiawatha Park in Oak Bluffs. Many members of the original landladies' families still maintain these properties today. Some will continue to operate them tomorrow and for years to come.

I sincerely hope the Trail continues to honor those who came before us and will dedicate more sites to honor the legacies of the African-Americans of Martha's Vineyard.

Carrie Camillo Tankard is the co-founder of the Heritage Trail and the first Vice-President of the Martha's Vineyard Chapter of the N.A.A.C.P. She is the keeper of the archives, chairperson of the annual Martin Luther King Day Dinner, and coordinates the activities of several other committees of the N.A.A.C.P. She has received several awards honoring her activism within the Island community.

INTRODUCTION

Elaine Cawley Weintraub

The African American Heritage Trail is a great source of pride to the community of color here on the Vineyard. It honors the achievements of African American people and acknowledges the painful past. It tells the whole story, describes the struggle and celebrates the victories. It has given us back our lost stories.

—Mandred Henry, president, Martha's Vineyard Chapter of the NAACP.

The African-American Heritage Trail is a physical entity consisting of a series of identified sites commemorating the history of people of color on Martha's Vineyard. Our adjunct nonprofit corporation which I founded with Carrie Camillo Tankard, vice-president of the Martha's Vineyard chapter of the NAACP, is formally identified as The African-American Heritage Trail History Project. The mission of the corporation is to research, disseminate and educate the community of Martha's Vineyard about the African-American history on the Island. Several sites have been identified and plaques celebrating the existence and achievements of individual people of color, placed at each one. There are 17 identified sites. The sophomore history classes of Martha's Vineyard Regional High School assist in archival research for the Heritage Trail, gather oral histories, create original art, and maintain the sites under my direction.

For me, education has been the transformative experience that allows me to understand some of the indignities and confusions that are part of the experience of a marginalized community. I have become aware that my experience is part of a larger question: What role do race, class and gender play in disempowering certain communities? The category of voice can only be constituted in differences, and it is in, and through, these multiple layers of meaning that students are positioned, and position themselves, in order to be the subject – rather than merely the object of history. (Aaronowitz and Giroux, 1993, p.100).

THE PROJECT BEGAN IN 1989

I began the work of researching the history of the African-American community of Martha's Vineyard in 1989. I was inspired to do so by the complete lack of any reference to that history in the school where I was employed. The catalyst to actually begin the work was a small boy who asked me: "Where were the black people then?" His question began my journey.

The original work was archival in that I explored old newspapers, shipping logs, reports, obituaries, bills-of-sale, probated wills and court records. I succeeded in documenting the life of an African-American whaling captain, William A. Martin, whose life had become shrouded in obscurity. By searching census records, wedding certificates and court files, I managed to uncover and document the lives of three remarkable women of his family. This research project examined the specific issue of enslavement, and discovered the lives of people of color whose experiences had not been documented or recorded.

ENSLAVEMENT ON MARTHA'S VINEYARD WAS DOCUMENTED

I began to research the question of enslavement on Martha's Vineyard after I found a copy of a bill-of-sale which confirmed the transaction of a ten-year-old "Negro boy" identified as Peter. According to a document that was part of a huge mass of uncatalogued papers at the Martha's Vineyard Museum, Zacheus Mayhew of Edgartown sold

Bill of sale for 10-year-old Negro boy, Peter

the boy to Ebenezer Hatch of Falmouth on June 19th, 1747. I pursued this line of inquiry by reading an article that had been published in the *Dukes County Intelligencer* in August, 1991. The article by Jacqueline Holland included a paragraph describing the inclusion of enslaved people in the wills of certain of the founding families of Martha's Vineyard. I searched the archives of the probate department of the town clerks' offices, and read several wills in which enslaved people were listed as part of the inventory of property.

Having confirmed the existence of enslavement on Martha's Vineyard, I began a detailed study of how that institution was established in the Massachusetts Bay Colony. I read widely among the diaries and journals of early English settlers to the Colony. Of particular significance to me was the work of Judge Samuel Sewall.

His 1700 essay "The Selling of Joseph" is considered the first definitive antislavery statement among the settlers. "Liberty," he states, "is the real value unto life and one ought not part with it themselves or deprive others of it, but upon mature consideration." (Sewall, 1700, from Moore, 1968, p. 83-87).

What emerged from my investigation is a rich history of African-American people. That history eventually became told by a series of plaques on the Heritage Trail. The physical entity of the African-American Heritage Trail has 17 dedicated sites. All are described here with a brief history of the research process that identified each.

The Trail is doing a great job educating people about the Island's African American history and supporting appreciation for diversity. Everything helps. The greatest value is that the Trail is in the schools because that is where so much work is needed. We need to hear all of the stories from all of the communities of this Island. We have heard only the story of the winners. We don't need to take anything away. We just need to add in more. We should struggle to find all of the lost histories and heroes and make them available.

—Adriana Ignacio, Tribal member, Wampanoag Tribe of Aquinnah

Know all men by these presents,
I, William A. Martin of Edgartown in the
County of Dukes County, and Commonwealth of
Massachusetts, being of sound and disposing
mind and memory, make publish and declare
this my last Will and Testament in manner
and form following that is to say,

First; I revoke all wills and codicils
hitherto made.

Second. I direct that all my debts and
funeral charges be paid.

Third. I give bequeath all and singular
the real and residue of my property, real
personal and mixed of which I may
die seized or possessed of every name
nature or description to my wife Sarah
G. Martin of said Edgartown.

Fourth. I also appoint the said Sarah G.
Martin, my wife, Executrix of this my will.

Witness this my hand and seal at
New Bedford in the County of Bristol and
said Commonwealth this Twenty Second
day of October, in the year Eighteen hundred
and seventy five

THE PROJECT BEGAN TO UNCOVER
STORIES NEVER TOLD BEFORE

The work of the Heritage Trail was based on the original research into the lives of William A. Martin and three generations of his maternal family. I received two Cuffe Fellowships from the Mystic Seaport Museum to help finance and encourage that scholarship. Mystic's mission is to support new research into the contributions of people of color to the maritime history of the New England. This research has revealed a family whose story begins with the brutality of enslavement and ends with the triumph of an African-American man who became the master of whaling ships from Edgartown and New Bedford.

William A. Martin was the only African-American whaling captain from Martha's Vineyard. He was the great-grandchild of a woman from Africa who was enslaved on Martha's Vineyard. His grandmother, born into enslavement, ended her life as a woman feared for her supernatural powers in the maritime community of Edgartown. His mother's life was difficult, and yet her son achieved remarkable distinction.

Despite the achievements of William Martin, his life story had never been told. It has been the mission of the Heritage Trail History Project to record the story of this family for posterity. That objective has been achieved.

The African-American Heritage Trail History Project has acted as a community education resource. We have archived

Will of Captain Martin

material, provided community celebration, published research and operated tours of the Heritage Trail. We have been supported in our work through donations, grants and the sale of the booklet *The African-American Heritage Trail*.

THE COMMUNITY GOT INVOLVED

The project has involved and excited the community, while providing the catalyst for a new interest in the contributions of people of color to the history of the Vineyard. One of the goals sought to build links between our various communities whose contributions have been undervalued.

The plaque at the Regional High School celebrates the achievements of the multicultural basketball teams, many of whose players were African American. The research undertaken into the Irish-born community on the Vineyard in the 1850s further built such cross-cultural bridges. We have worked within the community to gather stories and build collaborative relationships. The successful negotiations with the various town boards on the Island to dedicate specific sites are an example of sensitive, patient and respectful collaboration.

We have worked with the town of Edgartown to establish a site at the Memorial Wharf to honor the life of Nancy Michael. With the communities of Aquinnah and Chilmark we have dedicated two sites to commemorate the rescue of a fugitive from enslavement.

The plaque at the Regional High School celebrating the achievements of the basketball teams was placed there as a result of community interest in those teams. Many of the sites dedicated to the story of the community of color on this Island are on property owned by the Martha's Vineyard Land Bank. There has been widespread support for the Trail within the community since 1997, and we have received donations from several of the Island's banks, businesses and the local cultural councils.

A new idea is not always greeted with enthusiasm, and for some years it was difficult for the history project to grow within the high school. The expansion of the project would ensure that this remarkable history never again became lost or distorted.

Ironically, being denied support within the confines of the history department meant that the project depended upon the wider community. This led to an inclusive, dynamic and shared ownership of the Heritage Trail project which has greatly facilitated its growth. In recent years, the project has had the enthusiastic support of the principal and faculty. In 2004, the entire sophomore class has studied the story of Captain William A. Martin and the three generations of strong women who preceded him.

In every community, there are stories dimly remembered or lost in the margins of aged official documents. The Heritage Trail History Project is about finding those stories and giving them to our Island community. Our intention is to help build an inclusive history that speaks for all. Though the main focus of our story is the original research done into the lives of William

A. Martin and his family, we have also been involved in the researching of all of the diverse personal histories that make up the legacy of people of color on Martha's Vineyard.

THE TRAIL CONTINUES TO GROW
AND EDUCATE THE COMMUNITY

Since the establishment of the Trail in 1997, we have been a source of education for our community through publishing research in the Vineyard newspapers, celebrating each site dedication by inviting the public to attend and by building the Heritage Trail web site which is accessible world wide. The board of the Heritage Trail History Project has been fortunate enough to have been approached by people in our community anxious to share stories, photographs and recollections. We have commissioned a series of photographs of the Trail taken by Donalexander Goss, several of which are on display in the Dukes County Savings Bank in Oak Bluffs.

There is evidence of the presence of the Heritage Trail History Project in every town on Martha's Vineyard. The project has generated strong interest from several academic institutions throughout the country. The work of the sophomore students is displayed at the Martha's Vineyard Museum, and in the summer of 2004, several projects on the Trail were displayed at the Vineyard Steamship offices and local libraries. The involvement of the students lends a vitality to the project, and it is their enthusiastic participation and excitement that generates interest throughout the community.

Students who have a particular interest in the Trail retain their contact with it once their sophomore year is complete and act as tour guides for the incoming sophomore classes. There is also an education program provided by sophomore students for the Island grade schools. Several students have served on the board of the Heritage Trail History Project, and the Trail has recognized their contributions with scholarships when they graduate.

Jade Cash, Jarrett Campbell, Brian Scott
with Elaine Weintraub

Elaine Cawley Weintraub is the co-founder of the Heritage Trail a historian and history department chair at the Martha's Vineyard Regional High School. Her research work on the African American history of Martha's Vineyard has been published by the New England Journal of History, Mystic Seaport Museum and the Organization of American Historians. She was a Paul Cuffe Fellow for the years 1993 and 1996. This fellowship is granted by the Munson Institute at the Mystic Seaport Museum in recognition of original scholarship into the field of "minority contributions to the maritime history of New England."

A finalist for the Massachusetts Teacher of the Year program in 2001, she was Massachusetts Global Educator of the Year in 2003 and received an award from the World of Difference Anti-Defamation League in 1998 as a teacher who fights bigotry and prejudice. A fellow of the Massachusetts Teacher Leadership Academy, Elaine Cawley Weintraub was awarded her doctorate in Educational Leadership and Change in 2000. She is a board member of the Martha's Vineyard Chapter of the NAACP, Facing History & Ourselves Institute and the African American Heritage Trail of Martha's Vineyard.

"One's life has value as long as one attributes value to the lives of others by means of love, friendship, indignation and compassion.

-Simone de Beauvoir, French philosopher

In Loving Memory of George Van Buren Tankard
1934-2004

His humor and vision of what the Trail could be was a inspiration,
a source of strength and of much amusement.

Pulpit Rock

JOHN SAUNDERS — THE EXHORTER

Late 1700s

John preached with zeal

This is a chronicle of the experiences of African-American people on the Island of Martha's Vineyard in Massachusetts. This Island is steeped in the history of whaling, and its people have been sailors since the earliest times when the Native American people knew the land as Noepe. It is perhaps not coincidental that the story of the African-American people of Martha's Vineyard has two common themes: spirituality and maritime expertise. Water had a sacred significance in many West-African religions. Reverence for its power must have survived the horrors of the "Middle Passage"— crossing the Atlantic Ocean.

Religion has played a powerful role in the African-American community of Martha's Vineyard. On this Island, there were several black churches. African-Americans were closely involved with the development of both the Methodist and Baptist faiths on Martha's Vineyard. A prominent woman of

Pulpit Rock, nearby to the place, was used by preachers to spread the word of the Lord.

John Saunders, born into enslavement in Virginia, was a "pure African." His wife, Priscilla, was "half-white." They were transported to Martha's Vineyard by Captain T. Luce, hidden by corn. They were "zealous Christians."

John, being an exhorter, preached occasionally to the people of color at Farm Neck.

Site #6 on Heritage Trail — John Saunders

color, Nancy Michael, was believed to be a "professor of religion" in 19th century Edgartown.

JOHN SAUNDERS BRINGS METHODISM TO ISLAND

The connection between spirituality and the maritime world of New England is illustrated by the story of John Saunders, the preacher believed to have brought Methodism to Martha's Vineyard in 1787. According to a deposition taken from John Saunders' granddaughter, Mrs. Priscilla Freeman, Mr. Saunders "a pure African," and his wife Priscilla, who was "half-white" left Virginia where they were enslaved. Both were "zealous Christians."

They sailed with Captain T. Luce, "afterwards called the blind man." Captain Luce covered them with corn so that they would avoid detection. They arrived safely in Holmes Hole in Tisbury where they held several meetings. Colonel Davis later provided the couple with a home. A child was born to them also named John Saunders, a man referred to as "the celebrated singer and dancer." In 1793, John Saunders indentured one of his sons to Meleatiah Pease of Edgartown for a period of 20 years.

While living in Holmes Hole, Priscilla died, and John Saunders moved to Chappaquiddick Island to preach the word of God. In the words of his granddaughter he "preached with zeal and became acquainted with Jane Dimon and married with her, which exasperated the Indians there on account of his African descent." Intermarriage between African-Americans and Native Americans was not unusual so this statement about the Reverend Saunders' ethnic origin is surprising.

Mr. Saunders was apparently murdered on Chappaquiddick, and in other accounts religion is given as the reason. It seems likely that the Reverend Saunders' zealous preaching of Methodism was unwelcome to the Native American community of Chappaquiddick. Mr. Jeremiah Pease is quoted as saying that the Reverend Saunders was a martyr. (Deposition from Mrs. Priscilla Freeman, Martha's Vineyard Museum).

HE EXHORTED AT FARM NECK

It seems that John Saunders preached to the community of people of color in the Farm Neck area. "John being an exhorter (having it is understood held that position among his fellow slaves) preached occasionally to the people of color at Farm Neck." (Pease in Railton, 1983 p. 45).

A massive rock at the end of Pulpit Rock Way, Waterview Farms, County Road, Oak Bluffs, is the spot from which it is believed Saunders, and others, exhorted and preached the word of the Lord. In the nearby Farm Neck cemetery, another rock is said to have been used for the same purpose. The Heritage Trail has placed a stone marker nearby to the site of the Pulpit Rock on the property of the Land Bank. The stone marks a site on the Trail and honors the contribution to Vineyard history made by John Saunders, and other nameless preachers of color. The wording reads: "John, being an exhorter, preached to the people of color at this place."

Fugitive Slave Act

The Fugitive Slave Act of 1850 was a second attempt to effect compromise between the slave-owning and non-slave-owning states. The law was intended to broker the preservation of the Union. Under the terms of the law, any slave escaping to the north from the south was to be returned to the slave holder. Bounties were paid to any persons who apprehended runaways.

Although the specific targets under the strict application of the Fugitive Slave Act of 1850, were actually runaway slaves, in practice, this fee for capture led to a situation whereby free people of color in both the north and the south were vulnerable to kidnap by bounty hunters who sold them to slave holders.

Solomon Northrup, a free African-American from New York, was kidnapped and sold to a plantation owner in Louisiana where he remained enslaved for 12 years. His story was recorded in the *Narrative of Solomon Northrup* and is just one example of the vulnerability of people of color during this time. There are many stories of both false imprisonment and of people running away to the north, and one of those stories unfolded on the Vineyard.

RANDALL BURTON — THE RESCUE

1854

*He had resolved when he ran away the second time
that he would never be taken back alive, but
would instead die fighting for his freedom.*

In 1854, Randall Burton, a fugitive from enslavement, escaped from a ship in Holmes Hole in Tisbury and was rescued by "two women" who took him to a swamp in Gay Head. It appears that the Sheriff attempted to arrest Mr. Burton under the provisions of the Fugitive Slave Act of 1850, but he became "entranced" and was unable to make the arrest. (*Vineyard Gazette*, 1854). Mr. Burton escaped from Menemsha to New Bedford and later to Canada and freedom. According to an article published in the *Vineyard Gazette* on September 29, 1854, Randall Burton was being charged with larceny. This charge related to the stealing of a boat in which to make his escape from the bark, *Franklin*.

After the escape of the slave from the Franklin,
he landed on West Chop and proceeded to Gay

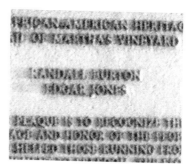

*Randall Burton
Site #2 — Tribal Land,
West Basin, Aquinnah
and Menemsha, Chilmark*

23

*Head where he entered a swamp and remained
concealed for several days. On the 16th, a warrant
was placed in the hands of Deputy Sheriff
Lambert of Chilmark for his arrest on a charge of
larceny, the offense alleged being the stealing of
a boat from the* Franklin. *With this warrant in his
pocket, Sheriff Lambert proceeded to search for
the slave. He went to Gay Head but did not enter
the swamp indeed he did not know, not having
been informed, at least positively, that the slave
was there. (Vineyard Gazette,* September 29,
1854).

The article describes how two women who were determined
to save him disguised Randall Burton in female garb, and hid
him in a swamp in Gay Head where Sheriff Lambert searched
for him.

*When the Sheriff entered the swamp, he was
'entranced,' he forgot his mission, the reins fell
from his hand, and he thought of nothing but
nature and music and the goodness of God.
When he aroused from his delightful trance, it
was to discover the tracks of the carriage and
the impression of human feet. But this discovery
came too late. As he made it the slave stepped
into the boat. (Vineyard Gazette,* September 29,
1854)

A letter to the editor of the *Vineyard Gazette* dated October 13th, 1854 disputes the version of events in their article, and defends the reputation of Sheriff Lambert.

I have some slight acquaintance with Deputy Sheriff Lambert and I should doubt if anyone ever saw his hand unnerved when he was obeying a law of his country with a warrant from good and lawful authority.

If Mr. Lambert had not had a prisoner at that time that must be disposed of according to law, it is my humble opinion that neither the heroic women or even the veritable writer of the article in the Gazette himself would have saved the thief from arrest.

Where, Mr. Editor, was the writer himself? In these perilous times was he skulking behind those females he should have led protected or was he laughing in his sleeve to think that to proclaim their deeds of valor would be glory enough for him. Mr. Editor, look at the case. He must have been the very man that could not be induced to enter the swamp since he knew all about it. Sir, the critter has not even the shadow of a gizzard in his breast much less the heart of a man. (*Vineyard Gazette*, October 13, 1854)

WERE RANDALL BURTON AND
EDGAR JONES THE SAME MAN?

There is another story about this rescue though a different name is used, namely Edgar Jones, but this story has many similarities to the version reported by the *Vineyard Gazette* in 1854. Though the names are different, it is generally believed that Edgar Jones and Randall Burton were the same person.

This story of the rescue was published in the *Vineyard Gazette* in 1921, and was told by Netta Vanderhoop of Aquinnah. In this version of events, the man fleeing from enslavement stowed away on a boat that came into Holmes Hole. His presence was discovered by the captain who told him to stay on the boat, and promised that he would not report him. In reality, the captain informed the Sheriff of the presence of the stowaway in hopes of receiving a share of the bounty payment.

Placque at Menemsha

Assisted by sailors on the boat, the fugitive was urged to flee and was dressed as a woman and taken to Aquinnah (then Gay Head). According to Mrs. Vanderhoop, her grandmother was the woman who hid Edgar Jones. She recalled her grandmother telling her that the Sheriff had come to Gay Head and offered ten dollars to anyone who would help him catch the fugitive.

According to Mrs. Vanderhoop, only one member of the tribe was tempted to take the money, and his opinion was overruled. Speaking of the fugitive, the article states that he (Edgar Jones) had "resolved when he ran away the second time that he would never be taken alive, but instead would die fighting for his freedom" (*Vineyard Gazette*, February 3rd, 1921). Mrs. Vanderhoop describes how the rescue was carried out through the active leadership of her grandmother, Mrs. Beulah Vanderhoop:

> *The men had outrun the Sheriff and when Mrs. Vanderhoop reached the spot where they were, that official was nowhere in sight. She told the young men that the man they were chasing was probably a slave and begged them not to help catch him. They gladly yielded to her wishes and were very indignant with the Sheriff for using a pretext in his attempt to make them slave catchers.* (*Vineyard Gazette*, February 3rd, 1921)

Mrs. Vanderhoop describes in her article how the Sheriff asked a little boy if he had seen a man run past. The child pointed to the place where the slave was hidden, and though the Sheriff saw the fugitive he did not dare attack him alone so "a watch was stationed in the tower of the lighthouse while he went to get his sons to help him effect the capture."

Escape of the Fugitive Esther

The *Vineyard Gazette* in its edition of June 2nd, 1854 describes another story relating to a fugitive from enslavement. In a deposition given by Thomas Taylor mate of the sloop *Endeavor* and George Edwards, John Flowers and James Fleet sailors on that vessel, the escape of a fugitive Esther identified as an "Indian woman" is described.

We brought her from Boston to carry to North Carolina to her master which we understood belonged unto Thomas Williams of said North Carolina. And on our passage, we put into the harbor at Edgartown on the twenty seventh day of July instant: and in the evening we bound her feet to a crowbar and tied her hands behind her, and put her down into the hold, and laid the hatches. How she got loose we know not; but in the morning she was gone with the sloop's long boat. Which Indian woman, we understood, came privately in sail sloop from North Carolina. And we were all on board but asleep when she went away, and knew

nothing of her going away. And we further knew that she was kept in the jail in Boston until we were ready to sail; and just before we sailed we went up to the jail, and fetched her down, and put her on board the above said sloop to convey her, as aforesaid, to the port of North Carolina to her said master.
(*Vineyard Gazette*, June 2nd, 1854)

It is apparent from this deposition that there was an inquiry into Esther's escape, and that the sailors who had been responsible for returning her to North Carolina were expected to explain their failure to do so. The account that they give seems a little suspect. If indeed Esther had been confined in the brutal manner that they describe, would it have possible for her to escape? The possibility exists that her jailors were negligent or that they were compassionate. Esther was not captured so whatever the real circumstances of her escape, she must have certainly been hidden somewhere on Martha's Vineyard.

Vineyard Gazette, February 3rd, 1921). Edgar Jones was successfully hidden and eventually taken to Menemsha where anonymous fisherman took him to New Bedford from where he was able to escape to Canada.

TWO SITES ARE DEDICATED

Elaine Cawley Weintraub and Serel Garvin at Aquinnah.

In 2001, the Heritage Trail dedicated two new sites to honor the story of Randall Burton and Edgar Jones who are widely believed to be the same person. The first site which was dedicated was on the Wampanoag Tribal Land at West Basin in Aquinnah in the presence of the entire Tribal Council.

The dedication took place to the sound of tribal drumming and the Wampanoag honor song. Speaking at the dedication, Adriana Ignacio of the Wampanoag Tribe

Menemsha School Third Graders at Aquinnah plaque.

William Vanderhoop, tribal elder and drummers Woody Vanderhoop, Jason Baird and David Vanderhoop at Aquinnah.

spoke of the bravery and selflessness of the tribal members who had risked so much to disobey an unjust law and save a stranger.

The rock, bearing a plaque honoring the Wampanoag Tribe for their part in the rescue, is on the tribal land at West Basin and faces Menemsha, the port from which the rescue was conducted A second plaque has been placed in Menemsha on a rock overlooking the water. The plaque pays tribute to the fishermen of Menemsha who saved the life of the fugitive.

SLAVE SHIP *AMISTAD* VISITS VINEYARD

On the same day that the two new Heritage Trail sites, in Aquinnah and Menemsha, were dedicated, the Heritage Trail hosted a visit to the Island from the vessel *Amistad*. Hundreds of Islanders waited on line to explore this vessel and learn the story of the *Amistad* rebellion. The *Heritage Trail History Project* arranged and coordinated the visit of the *Amistad* as part of our ongoing mission to provide education for our Island community about the experiences of people of African descent in the history of the United States.

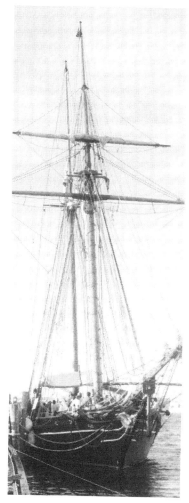

REBECCA, WOMAN FROM AFRICA

Died: 1801

*"She was called a slave all the time.
He used to whip her like a dog"*

The story of the experiences of people of African descent on this Island begins with the brutality of enslavement and ends with the triumph of an African-American man sailing as master of whaling ships out of Edgartown and New Bedford. The name of this man was William A. Martin, and he was the only African-American Whaling Captain from Martha's Vineyard. William A. Martin, who began his life in dire poverty, achieved the distinction of becoming the only African-American master of whaling ships on Martha's Vineyard. Born only one generation away from enslavement, he became a respected member of a sea faring community.

To understand the full extent of the success of William Martin, the only African-American master of whaling ships on Martha's Vineyard, it is necessary to reflect on the lives of his mother, grandmother and great-grandmother. Their experience included enslavement, imprisonment and the marginal existence of public paupers.

The story begins with a woman known as Rebecca or "Beck." She was William A. Martin's great-grandmother. Rebecca was born in Guinea in West Africa. She was taken from her home and endured the degradation and misery of the Middle Passage to live out her life as the property of Cornelius Bassett of Chilmark. Rebecca's life is shrouded in the mystery of the long gone and largely unrecorded past, but archival research has revealed pieces that help create a picture.

The information available tells the story of a life of cruel

Site #3 — Rebecca of Africa

servitude. I know that Rebecca had two sons, Pero and Cato, and one daughter, Nancy. It is possible she had other children. I can find no information on Cato's fate, but at the time of Colonel Bassett's death in 1779, Nancy aged 7 and Pero aged 18, were sold to Joseph Allen of Tisbury. Rebecca, their mother, was still alive at the time but she was not included in the inventory of property that listed her children. She may have been granted freedom at the time, but there is no record of her emancipation. Based on the evidence, it is a reasonable assumption that during her life Rebecca saw all of her children sold away as her master's property.

REBECCA MARRIED ISLAND WAMPANOAG

Rebecca was married at one time in her life to Elisha Amos. Information on Rebecca's life in Chilmark in part derives from a deposition given by a woman named Remember Cooper. The testimony was given during litigation between the Towns of Edgartown and Tisbury (SJC #6563 Barnstable). Remember's recollections of Rebecca's life in Chilmark were clear. When asked if she had known Elisha Amos, she replied affirmatively and noted that the "Indian man" and Rebecca at times lived as husband and wife. She specifically stated that Amos was not the father of Rebecca's daughter Nancy. This information is obviously correct because Amos died in 1763, nine years before the birth of Nancy.

Remember Cooper stated that Rebecca and Elisha Amos lived together part of the time. "I never knew they were married, they separated and got together again and he died then. She lived most of the time with Colonel Bassett. The place where Amos died was five or six miles from Colonel Bassett's."

When questioned as to Rebecca's status on Colonel Cornelius Bassett's estate, Remember Cooper responded: "She was called a slave all the time: he used to whip her like a dog. I have heard Colonel Bassett's boys call her a slave all the time."

Rebecca, "Woman of Africa" — born in Africa, and enslaved in Chilmark, she married Elisha Amos, a Wampanoag man. She was the mother of Nancy Michael. Rebecca died a free woman in this place in 1801.

Elisha Amos left a will (1/272 Dukes County Probate) that provided for his "beloved wife Rebecca." She received livestock and Amos's dwelling house for as long as she lived. Upon her death, the house reverted to his nephew. The land he possessed was willed to another nephew with the stipulation that he would provide hay for Rebecca annually. The disposition of property suggests that none of Rebecca's children were the children of Elisha Amos. It is possible that Rebecca's sons Pero and Cato were his children and that

he did not leave any inheritance to them because of their enslaved status. Before his marriage to Rebecca, Elisha Amos was previously married. Records show that he was married to Esther Nunneck on August 28, 1745. Zachariah Papamick performed the ceremony, and Experience Mayhew added translation.

ELISHA AMOS OWNED THE GREAT FIELD IN CHILMARK

Research at the Dukes County Registry of Deeds shows that Elisha Amos, described as an "Indian man and laborer" whose Indian name was Jonoxett, acquired much land during the 1740s and early '50s. His original dwelling place appears to have been Christiantown, then in Tisbury, but he bought land in Gay Head Neck and in Roaring Brook in Chilmark. He seems to have bought most of his land from other Native Americans and eventually had 80 acres in Chilmark in the area of Roaring Brook and the Great Field. The land is described in detail in a judgment given against Mr. Amos's neighbors on July 6, 1751.

In this case, Samuel Allen, yeoman, Ruth Hillman, widow, and Matthias Sheetup, Indian man and laborer, were found guilty of unjustly withholding or removing Mr. Amos from his Chilmark property. They were fined 8 pounds and 11 shillings, and ordered to pay an extra 2 shillings for damage to Mr. Amos's "goods and chattels" (Dukes Country Registry of Deeds). This property in Great Bight, North Chilmark was where Elisha Amos lived and this is where Rebecca lived with him "some of the time." The property of Cornelius Bassett, now known as the Flanders Farm, where Rebecca was enslaved, is about four miles away.

The Martha's Vineyard Land Bank has recently acquired land at Great Bight, North Road, Chilmark which includes the property owned by Elisha Amos. A map of the area prepared by the Land Bank shows that Rebecca Amos owned a field in that area until the time of her death in 1801. A story exists that Rebecca was the person who first saw Charles Grey's flagship, *Carysfort,* as it struggled through Quick's Hole during the 1778 raid on the Island during the Revolutionary War. The same map shows that Cooper owned the land adjoining Rebecca's field, presumably the family of Remember Cooper. The African-American Heritage Trail has placed a rock bearing a plaque honoring Rebecca, the woman from Africa, on the Land Bank property at Great Bight Reserve. This site is in a beautiful position at the beginning of the descent to the beach, and it has become a place where people leave rocks, shells and feathers to honor Rebecca.

Enslavement in New England

The institution of enslavement in New England is clouded with ambivalence. It certainly existed on Martha's Vineyard as it did elsewhere in the Commonwealth of Massachusetts. Some evidence suggests that Rebecca was "allowed" some freedom as witnessed by the relationship between her and Elisha Amos. Massachusetts law entitled her to inherit property. The property she inherited from Elisha Amos was for her lifetime only, but the stipulations of the will suggest that Mr. Amos did believe that Rebecca could live in his dwelling house.

More needs to be said about the peculiarities of enslavement in Massachusetts. Evidence is readily available showing that human beings were bought, sold and probated as property on Martha's Vineyard. Research at the Martha's Vineyard Museum uncovered a copy of a bill of sale from Zacheus Mayhew (1684-1760) of Edgartown to Ebenezer Hatch of Falmouth. The sale in question relates to Peter, a ten year old "Negro boy" to "have and to hold to the life of Ebenezer Hatch, his heirs, executors, administrators and assigns for ever." (Martha's Vineyard Museum archives.) The date of the bill of sale is June 19, 1747.

Governor Thomas Mayhew's grandson, Samuel Sarson, who died August 24, 1703, included in his estate "a Negro woman valued at 20 pounds." (Holland, 1991) In 1734, the estate of Ebenezer Allen of Chilmark included "Negroes" valued at "200 pounds along with two beds for servants, glasses, 1 pound 5 shillings, knives and forks at 18 shillings and 600 pair of sheep at 510 pounds and 17 shillings." (Ibid). Jane Cathcart of Chilmark, in June 1741, willed her "molato (mulatto) servant, Ismael Lobb, now in the service of Captain Timothy Daggett of Edgartown ... his freedom during life after he shall arrive at age 30." (Ibid). Cornelius Bassett's personal estate at the time of his death in 1779 included "one Negro boy, Pero, 33 pounds. One Negro woman, Chole (Chloe?) 27 years ... 150 pounds. One garl (girl), Nancy 7 years ... 180 pounds" (Dukes County Registry of Probate). Samuel Bassett of Chilmark owned land in both Chilmark and Edgartown. His will, probated in 1770 details his property listing one Negro woman, two boys ... 60 pounds .. pitchforks, scythes, rakes (Holland, 1991).

Puritan Massachusetts' ambivalent attitude toward the enslavement of African people is best illustrated by the antislavery tract: *The Selling of Joseph* written by Samuel Sewall in 1770. "Liberty," he states, "is the real value into life, and one ought not part with it

themselves or deprive others of it but upon mature consideration" (Higginbotham, 1978). Judge Samuel Sewall's statement was the first public antislavery statement even though enslaved Africans had been brought to Massachusetts Bay Colony since 1638. Mr. Sewall made several visits to Martha's Vineyard.

Some suggest that the Puritan settlers found slavery repugnant, but there is clear evidence that the Massachusetts Bay Colony settlers were deeply involved in the trade, and by the 1700s, New England was the most active slave trading area in America (Higginbotham, 1978). Martha's Vineyard would likely be similarly involved in the trading of enslaved people, and the documentation I have quoted shows that enslaved people were a part of the life of the Island. Despite the institution of enslavement, a significant development emerged in Massachusetts. At no time during its history did people of color lose the right to use the courts to challenge their status. Nor did they lose the right to inherit property in certain circumstances.

"Liberty is the real value into life, and one ought not part with it themselves or deprive others of it but upon mature consideration"

— Judge Samuel Sewall

NANCY MICHAEL
"A WOMAN OF POWER"

1772-1856

*"May her good deeds live long in our remembrance,
and her evil be interred with her bones"*

Colonel Cornelius Bassett died in 1779, and following his death, Rebecca's daughter Nancy was sold in 1779 to Joseph Allen of Tisbury. She was seven years old. Nancy did not disappear into obscurity. Her story is one of grueling hard times, enslavement, legal problems, public pauperism, and eventually a position of influence in the maritime community of Edgartown.

At this time, Nancy became known as Nancy Michael. The origin of the name Michael is unclear. Another Michael with the given name Caesar had a connection with the Bassett estate in Chilmark. In 1789, Nathaniel Bassett of Chilmark was appointed the guardian of Caesar Michael, "a mulatto boy." His authority as guardian was to protect the property rights that Caesar had inherited from his mother until the boy

*Nancy Michael:
A most singular
character.*

Site #17 — Nancy Michael

reached the age of 14 (Dukes County Registry of Probate). The possibility exists that Caesar was related to Nancy Michael. Caesar Michael married Elizabeth Sectom in Edgartown in 1797 (Edgartown Vital Records). Another connection exists with the name Michael. On December 20, 1819, Nancy Michael, "spinster, sister and only surviving heir to James Michael," conveyed land inherited from her brother to Isaiah D. Pease of Edgartown for $10.00 (Dukes Country Registry of Deeds 21/72).

Research by R. Andrew Pierce published in the Dukes County *Intelligencer* states that Nancy's father was Sharper Michael, an enslaved African who was the first Vineyarder to be killed by the British in the American Revolution, in 1777. Pierce quotes evidence that in 1804 and 1808 Nancy Michael sued two different men for financial support of her two children. She claimed that her daughters, Lucy and Rebecca, had been conceived at her brother James's house in Edgartown. In 1804 she referred to her brother as James Sharper and in 1808, James Michael. Based on this evidence, it is reasonable to conclude that Nancy's father was Sharper Michael, son of an African woman, Rose, who was enslaved by Zacheus Mayhew.

KNOWN AS "BLACK NANCE," NANCY MICHAEL HAD SKILLS AS A "CONJURE WOMAN"

Nancy Michael lived a long life. Following her sale to Mr. Joseph Allen in 1779, he "held and used her as a slave for a series of years" (SJC #6563 Barnstable). She "fell into distress in Edgartown in 1812" (ibid) The Town of Edgartown eventually brought suit against the Town of Tisbury in 1851 to claim reimbursement for money spent to support Nancy Michael, a public pauper. In the view of Edgartown, Nancy was the responsibility of the Town of Tisbury because she had been enslaved in that town. The case was heard at the Superior Court in Barnstable in 1852. The verdict was taken for the defendant, Tisbury, who had claimed that Nancy had never in fact been enslaved because slavery was no longer legal in the Commonwealth of Massachusetts at the time of her alleged enslavement. A previous court action had been taken by Edgartown in 1813 to force Tisbury to pay for the maintenance of one of Nancy's children born about 1810. Judgment had been rendered against Tisbury in 1813, but a fire had destroyed all records of the Court in Barnstable in 1827.

Nancy's obituary published in the *Vineyard Gazette* in 1857 presents a picture of a complex woman. The obituary states that Nancy was "naturally possessed of kind feelings, she was very fond of children and unusually attentive to their wants." This seems at variance with

An Old Landmark Gone

Mrs. Nancy Michael known to most of our readers by the familiar cognomen of Black Nance is no more. She departed this life on Saturday last, at a very advanced age. Probably she was not far from 100 years old. She had changed but little in her appearance for 40 years past, and those who knew her 50 years ago looked upon her as an old woman.

She was a very remarkable character in her day. Naturally possessed of kind feelings, she was fond of children and unusually attentive to their wants, and there are but few among us who have not at some time been indebted to her.

Possessed of a strong natural mind, she acquired great influence over some of our people, by many of whom she was looked upon as a witch. She professed to have the power of giving good or bad luck to those bound on long voyages; and it was no unusual thing for those about to leave on whaling voyages to resort to her, to propitiate her favor by presents and etc., before leaving home.

Special woes were denounced by her upon those who were too independent to acknowledge her influence. In case of bad news from any vessel commanded by one who had defied her power, she was in ecstasies, and her fiendish spirit would at once take full control of her. At such times, she might be seen in our streets, shaking her long, bony fingers at all unbelievers in her magical power and pouring forth the most bitter invectives upon those she looked upon as her enemies.

Her strange power and influence over many, continued till the day of her death, though for two or three years past she was mostly confined to her room. Taking her all in all, she was a most singular character, and it will doubtless be a long time before we shall look upon her like again. She was a professor of religion and we believe at one time adorned the profession. May her good deeds live long in our remembrance, and her evil be interred with her bones.

Vineyard Gazette, January 2, 1857

the later statement that she was "possessed of a strong natural mind, she acquired great influence over some of our people, by many of whom she was looked on as a witch."

It is stated that Nancy professed to have the power to give good or bad luck to those about to leave on long whaling voyages. Mariners about to leave on a whaling voyage sought her protection before leaving, and those who did not incurred her wrath. The obituary states that "in case of bad news from any vessel commanded by one who had defied her power, she was in ecstasies, and her fiendish spirit would at once take full control of her."

It is a fascinating and paradoxical picture of the woman, Nancy Michael. She obviously performed a service and profited from the gifts of superstitious sailors. It may be that she practiced the religion of her ancestors, including the emphasis on the supernatural element of water. It is quite likely that she may have learned the traditional rituals of the conjure woman from her mother. Perhaps she was mentally disturbed or shrewd enough to feign mental disturbance for her own ends. It seems likely that she used the skills of a "conjure woman" as a strategy to gain advantages for her family.

What is perfectly clear from the wording of the obituary is that Nancy Michael was feared in the seafaring community of Edgartown, and that she had a position of influence over the sailors. The obituary refers to her as "Black Nance" and states that her appearance had changed very little in 40 years and that "those who knew her 50 years ago knew her as an old woman." The obituary concludes: "Her strange power and influence over many continued until the day of her death, though for two or three years past she was mostly confined to her room. Taking her all in all she was a most singular character, and it will doubtless be a long time before we shall look upon her like again. She was a professor of religion, and we believe at one time adorned the profession. May her good deeds live long in our remembrance, and her evil be interred with her bones."

The 1855 State Census shows Nancy living in the home of Charles and Julia Vincent in Edgartown. There are five elderly women listed as living in their home, and four of them were white. The probable explanation is that the Vincent family was paid by the town to provide a home for these impoverished women, all of whom are referred to as public paupers. There was no building in Edgartown specifically designated as a home for paupers.

The Heritage Trail dedicated a site to the memory of Nancy Michael at the Memorial Wharf in Edgartown where one can stand and see Chappaquiddick Island. The wording reads: "Nancy Michael — a most singular woman."

REBECCA MARTIN

1809-1854

Nobody knows the trouble I've seen

Nancy Michael had a daughter, Rebecca, born in 1808 or 1809. Rebecca was the mother of Captain William A. Martin. There is incomplete information about Rebecca, but I know that in 1820, Rebecca was found guilty in a court case and was sentenced for 20 days. At the time of her imprisonment she would have been 11 years old.

This brief story offers some insights into Rebecca's life. Research by Arthur Railton published in the *Dukes County Intelligencer* shows that Rebecca was imprisoned in the Dukes County Jail on two occasions. Interestingly, the records show that the complainant against Rebecca on charges of theft and nonpayment of debt was her mother, Nancy Michael. (*Dukes County Intelligencer*)

Further research into the records of the Dukes County House of Corrections held at the Martha's Vineyard Museum shows that throughout her life Rebecca was imprisoned for short

Nobody knows the trouble I've seen

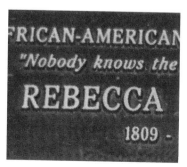

Site #12 — Rebecca Martin

Nobody Knows the Trouble I've Seen

Nobody knows the trouble I've seen. Nobody knows but Jesus.
Nobody knows the trouble I've seen, glory hallelujah.

Sometimes I'm up, sometimes I'm down, oh yes Lord,
sometimes I'm almost on the ground, oh yes Lord,

Nobody knows the trouble I've seen but Jesus.
Nobody knows the trouble I've seen, glory hallelujah.

One day when I was walking along, oh yes, lord.

periods. On occasion she spent several months incarcerated because she was unable to make the appropriate payments. In 1838, she was imprisoned following a complaint of assault by her mother, Nancy Michael.

Even for young children, short sentences in the House of Corrections for petty crimes were the norm: "On September 18, 1851, William H. Charles, a boy of nine or ten years of age, was committed for an assault and battery on the body of Susan O. Sylvia, a girl of about the same years of age. Sentenced for two days" (Dukes County House of Corrections records, Martha's Vineyard Museum).

The sky opened up and love came down, oh yes lord,

Nobody knows the trouble I've seen but Jesus.
Nobody knows the trouble I've seen, glory hallelujah.

What made ole Satan hate me so? Oh yes Lord.
He had me once and let me go, oh yes Lord.

Nobody knows the trouble I've seen but Jesus.
Nobody knows the trouble I've seen, glory hallelujah.

I shall never forget that day, oh yes lord,
when Jesus washed my sins away. Oh yes Lord.

WILLIAM MARTIN IS BORN
TO REBECCA MICHAEL

In 1830, Rebecca Michael gave birth to a son, William A. Martin. She used the name Martin, but it is not clear who was the father of the child. Many years later, Captain Martin's wife, Sarah, gave the information that her husband's father had also been a William A. Martin, but she did not know where he had been born. On Captain Martin's marriage certificate in 1857, he gave only one parent's name and that was Rebecca Francis (New Bedford Public Library Genealogy Project). The use of the name Francis is explained by the fact that in 1831, Rebecca Martin of Chilmark married John Francis of New York in Edgartown (Edgartown Vital Records). From that time, Rebecca used the name Francis but she was also referred to as Michael.

John Francis's name also appears in the records of the Dukes County House of Corrections. In 1828, he was committed to jail for assault and battery on Tristan Swain, but was discharged the same day. On November 16th in 1831, he was committed to jail "for safe keeping" and was discharged on November 21st of the same year by the payment of costs and a fine (Dukes County House of Corrections records, Martha's Martha's Vineyard Museum). The practice of "safe keeping" was a common strategy to prevent sailors from jumping ship. The seamen were released from incarceration when the ship was ready to begin its voyage.

Jeremiah Pease, a man who was involved in the life of the community of Martha's Vineyard, kept diaries that recorded the daily events of life on the Island. An entry dated October 29, 1854 states that he attended meetings at Eastville. His diary records that "Rebecca, a coloured woman died. She was the daughter of Nancy Michael aged about 50 years. She died about 8 a.m."

At the time of her death, William Martin was sailing as first mate and keeper of the log on the whaling vessel the *Europa*. Mr. Pease was a very enthusiastic Methodist, and perhaps Rebecca was a member of his church. It seems significant that Mr. Pease felt Rebecca's passing was important enough to record and that he mentioned her relationship to Nancy Michael. Nancy survived her daughter.

THE HERITAGE TRAIL PROJECT RESTORED THE OLD MARINE CEMETERY ON THE LAGOON IN OAK BLUFFS

The Heritage Trail History Project recently restored the Old Marine Cemetery adjacent to the State Lobster Hatchery on Shirley Avenue in Oak Bluffs. The small burial ground is Rebecca's likely final resting place. With community support, and with the assistance of the sophomore classes at Martha's Vineyard Regional High School, the once abandoned cemetery is now one of the most significant stops on the Heritage Trail.

When first identified, the cemetery was overgrown and eroded by flooding tides. The site itself was being used to store equipment belonging to the State Lobster Hatchery, and large water tanks blocked the entrance into the burial ground. The History Project began a campaign of letter writing to local officials and met with the state environmental agencies to bring attention to the plight of the cemetery. The water tanks were removed by order of the Commonwealth, and with the help of the staff of the Lobster Hatchery, and with community volunteers, a clean up campaign was successfully launched.

The Brian Murphy family of Tisbury were very involved in a landscaping project at the cemetery. With the family's generosity and the dedication of the sophomore history classes, gravestones are now restored, trees and flowers planted and a fence built behind which equipment belonging to the Lobster Hatchery can be stored out of view. The restoration work on the cemetery was featured on the WCVB Channel 5 Boston award-winning program, *Chronicle*.

Brian and Patrick Murphy at the Old Marine Cemetery

REBECCA MARTIN IS MEMORIALIZED THERE

The Heritage Trail has chosen to dedicate the Old Marine Cemetery to the memory of Rebecca Martin. A lone bench marks her memory with a plaque simply stating: "Nobody knows the troubles I've seen"— Rebecca Martin 1810-1854.

The 1850 census of Edgartown shows Nancy Michael, Rebecca Francis and William Martin living as a family unit in Edgartown. They did not own the property in which they lived. Nancy did not die until 1857, the year William Martin married Sarah Brown. From this background William Martin rose to achieve prominence in the maritime world of Martha's Vineyard. He, and the women of his family, did not accept the limitations placed upon them by their ethnicity in that period of history. Theirs is a remarkable story in which the love of the sea and the power of the spirit are intimately entwined.

CAPTAIN WILLIAM A. MARTIN

1830-1907

"Farewell to thee for a time, day's lingering sun is over."

William A. Martin, was the only African-American whaling captain from Martha's Vineyard. He was the great-grand child of a woman from Africa enslaved on Martha's Vineyard. His grandmother, born into enslavement, ended her life as a woman feared for her supernatural powers in the maritime community of Edgartown. William A. Martin, who began his life in dire poverty, achieved the distinction of becoming the only African-American master of whaling ships on Martha's Vineyard. Born only one generation away from enslavement, he became a respected member of a sea faring community.

He was born in Edgartown in 1830. His mother's name was Rebecca, and she was about 20 years old at the time of his birth. He lived with his mother and his grandmother, Nancy, in Edgartown and became involved in the maritime trade. He married Sarah Brown, a Native American woman from the Chappaquiddick Plantation. The Edgartown 1850 census

Site #9 — William A. Martin on Heritage Trail

shows Sarah Brown, then 18 years old, living as a maid in the Morse family home in Edgartown. In 1857, following the voyage of the whaleship *Europa* on which he sailed as keeper of the log, William Martin married Sarah Brown at the Baptist Church on Martha's Vineyard. They made their home with her family on the Chappaquiddick Plantation.

Captain Martin and Sarah lived in the Chappaquiddick Plantation which was the area of Chappaquiddick Island regarded as Indian land. *A Report to the Governor and Council* by John Milton Earle of 1861 commented on life there. The official attitude of racism toward Native American people at this time would obviously color the perceptions of those gathering the information, but it is clear enough that life on Chappaquiddick Plantation during the early years of William and Sarah Martin's marriage was extremely difficult.

SAILING WAS ONLY WAY PEOPLE OF COLOR COULD MAKE A LIVING

Despite poverty, the seafaring community of Chappaquiddick did have some advantages uncommon among seamen of color. The most significant was land ownership which meant that they could live in a somewhat settled and supportive community. Sailing was the only way that the Native Americans and other people of color could make a living since the expansionism of their white neighbors resulted in a constant loss of their lands.

The official attitude of racism toward Native American people at this time would obviously color the perceptions of those gathering the information for the 1861 report to the governor, but it is clear enough that life on Chappaquiddick Plantation during the early years of William and Sarah Martin's marriage was extremely difficult.

The Chappaquiddick Plantation

   Captain Martin and Sarah lived in the Chappaquiddick Plantation which was the area of Chappaquiddick Island regarded as Indian land. *A Report to the Governor and Council* by John Milton Earle of 1861 indicates that although this was a Native American community, people of other ethnicities lived there. Attached to the report is a list which describes the ethnicity of each person living in the community.

Abraham Brown (Sarah's father):   "mixed for'ner"

James W. Curtis: "colored for'ner," mariner of Edg.

John Ross: "colored for'ner," mariner & farmer

William Johnson: "colored for'ner," state pauper

William A. Martin: "colored for'ner," mariner

William H. Matthews: "colored for'ner, light boat keeper - away, supposed dead"

John E. West: "colored for'ner," barber of New Bedford

   All other persons listed are defined by their Native American ethnicity. A Native American community existed on Chappaquiddick Island until the 20th century, though now only one Native American family still lives there.

Life in that community could be quite difficult. A Report to the Governor on the Condition of the Indians of the Commonwealth dated 1861 indicates that land was held in "severalty," while an appointed guardian directed community affairs. The report recommended continuing the guardianship though it expressed some sympathy for the Native American community. Reference is made to the role of the guardian. Members of the community could not "sue or be sued without the consent of the guardian, could not receive wages for any voyage if payment be forbidden by the guardian, may be sent to sea as 'habitual drunkards, vagabonds and idlers' and their wages withheld by the guardian, and cannot under any circumstances alienate their lands or any portion of them." The author of the report made the point that such restrictions "may mostly be necessary; still in the hands of a guardian disposed to abuse such powers they might become insupportably oppressive to the Indians."

Concern is expressed about the extremely high death rate of the community on Chappaquiddick and reference is made to a Commissioners' Report of 1849 which found the location to be healthy. The report of 1861 states that "without any fatal epidemic having been among them, they dwindle away and disappear. The sea-faring life, which nearly all the men follow, to a greater or lesser extent is, unquestionably, unfavorable to the increase of the population, but it is not sufficient to account for the diminution that has occurred." The author of the Report offers three "satisfactory" reasons for this mortality:

1. The comparatively sudden change from the habits and modes of living of barbarous life to those of civilization, without waiting for the progressive physical and mental development which takes place when the process is more gradual, and which would adapt them to the change.

2. The habits of intemperance and licentiousness which always for a time, follow the contact of civilized and barbarous races, which not only carry off their victims prematurely, but so far impair the constitutions of their immediate descendants, as to make them more vulnerable to the ravages of disease.

3. The destitution, want and suffering, resulting from poverty which operate so powerfully to increase mortality in all the lower walks of life.

(*Report to the Governor and Council, on the Condition of the Indians*, John Milton Earle, 1861).

"Farewell to thee for a time,
day's lingering sun is over,
this heart will never awaken...
to one bright moment
more the hope...cherished here
within day by day
through life's flow."

In 1805, the "Indian natives and colour'd people inhabiting the Indian lands" on Chappaquiddick complained that "they consider [themselves] injured and oppress'd by many of the white inhabitants of Said Island" (Bolster, 1997).

The late Mr. Milton Jeffers, an oral historian and one of the last surviving members of the Chappaquiddick community, also made reference to the high mortality rate that prevailed within that community. He conceded the point about the dangers of the sea-faring life and the ravages of extreme poverty, but adds another dimension to the discussion. He recalled his mother mentioning "that people would become sick and start to cough, and then become too weak to leave the house and shortly after they would die." (Jeffers in Weintraub, 1993). His belief, and that of his community, was that they were extremely vulnerable to "white" diseases such as tuberculosis and other infections all of which had a decimating effect on them. (Jeffers in Weintraub 1993). The insight into the difficulties of the life of the Native American community on Chappaquiddick offered by this report coupled with the documented experiences of three generations of his family, give us some understanding of the remarkable achievements of Captain William A. Martin.

WILLIAM MARTIN IS KEEPER OF THE LOG

In October of 1853, when the *Europa* sailed from Edgartown, The master was John H. Pease and the keeper of the log was William A. Martin. The voyage ended on June

[illegible] Benny

Farewell by thee forsaken
[illegible] lingering was is over
[illegible] only never awaken [illegible]
[illegible] bright moment more the hope
[illegible] soul had cherished here withered
[illegible] though lifes flowers

24, 1857. A drawing of the house in which Sarah and Captain Martin made their home can be found in the *Europa's* journal and log book kept by Martin during the 1853 voyage on which he served as both first mate and keeper of the log. He obviously had great artistic talent demonstrated not only because of the remarkable accuracy of his rendition of Sarah's home but by many other wonderfully elaborate drawings of whales, sometimes as many as six or seven on a page. It seems likely that the house was Sarah Brown's family home before the marriage. Above the drawing, William Martin wrote:

"Farewell to thee for a time, day's lingering sun is over, this heart will never awaken... to one bright moment more the hope... cherished here within day by day through life's flow."

Some of the words are impossible to decipher on the microfilm, but clearly William Martin was distraught to be leaving the Island of Martha's Vineyard and the home of his beloved Sarah Brown. Whaling voyages were long, and conditions were very poor, so it is very likely that the young man was feeling both lonely and apprehensive as he began his voyage. William Martin wrote with a very fine hand, and obviously enjoyed writing. On the title page, he experimented with several styles and decorated the lettering.

WILLIAM MARTIN IS WHALING CAPTAIN FOR 30 YEARS

William A. Martin is listed as joint master and keeper of the log book with Thomas E. Fordham of the *Eunice H. Adams* on a voyage to the North Atlantic from October 16, 1867 to March 18, 1870 (whaling log books and journals). He captained the *Emma Jane,* an 86-ton schooner on her voyage to the Atlantic whaling grounds. The voyage began on October 9, 1883 and he returned on March 27, 1884 with 140 tons of sperm oil (Starbucks). He captained the *Golden City* out of New Bedford in 1878, and in 1887 the *Eunice H. Adams* out of Edgartown. His was a long and successful career spanning more than 30 years.

WILLIAM AND SARAH CELEBRATE THEIR 50ᵀᴴ WEDDING ANNIVERSARY

On July 2, 1907, Captain Martin and his wife Sarah celebrated their 50th wedding anniversary, which was recorded in the *Vineyard Gazette* of July 11, 1907. The tribute to Captain and Mrs. Martin is cordially worded, and it appears that they were held in high regard by the Edgartown community.

The article praises Captain Martin's whaling skills and refers to his early voyages on the *Almira* and *Europa* of Edgartown. He sailed for the agents Samuel Osborne, Jr. and Son, as first officer of the bark *Clarice* and master of the *Emma Jane.* It appears that his last voyage was in command of the *Eunice H. Adams.* The writer makes reference to the fact that "Captain Martin has been a paralytic for the past seven years and is now practically helpless."

The tribute poignantly concludes: "To all those who remember Captain Martin as he appeared some 25 years ago, and recall his quick, alert movements and crisp decisive speech, qualities which went far to make a successful whale man, it is difficult to realize his utter helplessness at the present time and he has the deep sympathy of all in the community" (*Vineyard Gazette*, July 11, 1907).

CAPTAIN MARTIN'S LEGACY

It is clear that Captain Martin was enormously successful in the maritime community of Martha's Vineyard. His skills as a "whale man" were deeply appreciated in a community that held such skills in very high regard. It is difficult across the gulf of time to make a judgment on how delicate a line William Martin stepped. He did not live in Edgartown among the grandiose homes of the other whaling captains, but in a modest house on a Native-American plantation on Chappaquiddick. His success did not challenge the social organization of an Island where, despite some apparent racial harmony, restrictive covenants relating to race and religion were placed on many property deeds. (Research, Registry of Deeds, Edgartown).

During the years of their marriage, his wife worked as a housekeeper for the Pease family of Edgartown where she was praised for the quality of soap that she made (Interview, Penny Williams, descendant of Sarah Brown). The Pease family seem to have played a significant role in the lives of William Martin and Sarah Brown. It is from the diaries of Jeremiah Pease that I have found valuable information about William Martin's mother and grandmother, and Martin sailed as keeper of the log on the vessel *Europa* under John H. Pease as master. Other members of the Pease family were involved in the surveying of the Chappaquiddick Plantation where Capt. Martin and Sarah lived.

CAPTAIN MARTIN AND SARAH ARE
BURIED ON CHAPPAQUIDDICK

They are buried in a Chappaquiddick graveyard where their grave stone, though an expensive one, faced the opposite way from most of the rest of the stones in the graveyard. In recent years, following public interest in the grave, the stone has been turned around.

There has been much speculation about why the gravestone faced the way that it did, and ideas have ranged from the notion that William Martin loved the sea and wanted visitors to his grave to be able to see it to the idea that in the burial grounds of that era people of color were placed in the corners away from other graves.

Site #5 — Captain Martin gravesite

Buried the wrong way?

We drove down a bumpy dirt road and stopped
in a small graveyard. As I walked onto the land, I
heard the crashing of the waves against the shoreline
abutting the graveyard. Surrounded by forest on three
sides and ocean on the fourth it seemed to me like a
little piece of heaven. I sat down on a stone bench in
the shade. It was then that I first saw it. The peculiar
difference of the grave which we had come to see.
The grave of whaling captain William A. Martin. The
grave was facing the wrong direction. By that I mean,
when you walk into the graveyard Captain Martin's
grave was the only one which could not be identified.
It had an inscription, two in fact. The first was the
name of William Martin and the second was his Native
American wife, Sarah Brown. It was not whether or
not it had an inscription though. It was the direction in
which the inscription was facing. Why was it that this
was the only grave that could not be identified from
the entrance of the cemetery?

At first I approached this question with an open
mind. "It is probably to stop the erosion from ruining
the inscription," I commented. "Maybe it was a
custom of the time." No. I went home that night and
looked for a Native-American or African-American

ritual that said one must be buried in such a way that you cannot be identified from the entrance to the graveyard. I was not at all surprised to find that no such custom existed. So I then looked at the photographs that I had taken only to see that a large percentage of the graves were facing the water. It had not been done to combat erosion.

I then knew exactly what had occurred. What had happened was that I was being naive. I knew then that there was no erosion plan or sacred custom dealing with this, but I wish that there had been. I now live with the conclusion that William Martin and his wife were facing the wrong direction because he was born black at the wrong time. Which is not to say that I ever feel that it's the wrong time to be born whoever you are, but there are always people who think that anyone born different from them has no right to be born at all. At the time of William Martin there were too many of these people.

As it turned out nothing on the tour would move me more than the old stone grave of the Vineyard's first black whaling captain, William Martin.

—Excerpted from "The Grave Not Seen," Erin Palacios, 1996

HERITAGE TRAIL PROJECT PUBLISHED CAPTAIN MARTIN'S LIFE

The African-American Heritage Trail History Project published the history of Captain William A. Martin's life in a booklet to which students contributed (Weintraub, 1997). One student wrote an essay reflecting on Captain Martin's gravestone while another contributed a portrait of the captain based on archival descriptions. There were no photographs of him.

In recent years, much publicity has been given to the campaign by the African-American Heritage Trail History Project to buy the Martin house which is in a very poor state of repair, and has been unoccupied for the past several years. Despite strong interest in the Island community, and several generous donations, the Heritage Trail History Project has not yet been able to acquire the house. Though no plaque has yet been placed at the Martin house or in the Chappaquiddick Cemetery, both of those places are widely recognized as sites on the Heritage Trail.

Amy Rogers, Danielle Ponte and Keenan Chaplin at the Martin House

CAPTAIN WILLIAM A. MARTIN

The first African American Whaling Captain.
MARTHA'S VINEYARD

The Shearer Cottage

1903

New England Cod Fish Cakes and Southern Rolls

In 1997, the Heritage Trail dedicated its first site, the Shearer Cottage on Rose Avenue in the Highlands area of Oak Bluffs. The Shearer is currently the property of Doris Jackson whose grandfather was Charles Shearer, the man who gave his name to the property.

CHARLES SHEARER WAS BORN INTO ENSLAVEMENT

Charles Shearer was born in Virginia where he was enslaved. Family oral history tells that during the Civil War, he ran away to join the Union Army. He was caught by the slaver holder, however, whipped, and tied up in the barn. The Union Army was advancing rapidly, and the plantation owner's family fled south leaving Mr. Shearer in the barn. Whether he was left behind deliberately or in the haste of flight is not known. Shearer was liberated by the Union Army and sent to the Hampton Institute, a school established for Native Americans and African-Americans. He graduated

Charles Shearer was born into slavery in Appomattox, Virginia. In 1880, he graduated from Hampton Institute and served on the faculty for 12 years. Later, Charles and his wife, Henrietta, purchased two homes — in Everett, MA and Oak Bluffs adjacent to the Baptist Campground. For many years, friends and family were invited to vacation with the Shearers. The concept of the first inn welcoming African-Americans on Martha's Vineyard was born in the 1920s. Shearer Cottage, famous for fine food and warm hospitality was visited by guests from all over the country and became the center of African-American activities on the Island.

Site #6 — Shearer Cottage

from Hampton, and remained there as a teacher until he was 30 years old. He met his wife-to-be, Henrietta, at Hampton. She was a member of the Blackfoot tribe, and a student at the institute. Together they came north, and Mr. Shearer became a waiter at the Parker House Hotel in Boston. The couple soon bought a house in Everett, Massachusetts.

Charles Shearer was a religious Baptist and an elder of the church. With his connection with the Baptist church, he eventually came to the Vineyard and bought his house from the Baptist church. The house adjoins the former Baptist Tabernacle now known as Temple Park in the Highlands area of Oak Bluffs. For a number of years, the house was operated as a residence and laundry.

SHEARER COTTAGE HOSTS
DISTINGUISHED AFRICAN-AMERICANS

After Henrietta Shearer's death, her daughters Sadie and Lily opened the house as an inn that catered for guests of color. In the years that followed, the Shearer Cottage became a favored place for many distinguished African-Americans.

Adam Clayton Powell and
Martin Luther King, Jr.

The cottage guest books are filled with names such as Paul Robeson, Harry Burleigh, Reverend Adam Clayton Powell and Ethel Waters. Harry Burleigh was a renowned singer who performed around the world for dignitaries such as Edward VII of England. Burleigh would spend summers at the Shearer writing down thousands of black spiritual songs. These songs had been preserved through the oral tradition. Were it not for Mr. Burleigh's years of cataloguing, many of America's most famous spiritual songs would have been lost. Among the songs he recorded for posterity were: "Deep River" and "Nobody Knows the Trouble I've Seen."

Harry Burleigh, 1918

The Shearer was truly a family operation, with each member taking a part. Doris Jackson recalls that the evening meal was served in one large room while she and her sisters waited on the tables. "We all worked hard and relied on each other. We were proud to be black and proud to be who we were" (Interview Doris Jackson, 1997). Mrs. Jackson's brother, Lincoln Pope, was the first African-American to be elected to the Massachusetts legislature when he was chosen as representative for Roxbury in 1956.

CHARLES SHEARER'S GRANDDAUGHTER REMEMBERS

Another sibling, the late Elizabeth White, spoke on the issue of identity and community in an interview in 1991.

> *After they moved to Massachusetts my grandfather, Charles Shearer, became the head waiter at the Parker House hotel. I believe that they came to the Vineyard because my grandmother had some kind of connection with the Native American community in Gay Head*

Lee Van Allen, Shearer's great-granddaughter, and current owner of the Shearer Cottage

[Aquinnah]. I remember them hiring a bus and taking about 15 family members up to Gay Head to see the Devines and the Vanderhoops. We all worked so hard to make the Shearer Cottage a success — and it was — because we believed in and supported each other.

As a community, we worked hard and struggled, but we always had hope that we would be accepted and valued for who we were. I remember Congressman Adam Clayton Powell very well. He was a really effective politician, but he never got the credit for all that he did. When he was chairman of the House Education and Labor Committee, he got 60 civil rights bills enacted. He opened up the bus employees union in New York City to African-Americans. His strategy was to boycott the buses from 110th Street in New York, and he recommended that strategy to the African-American community in Montgomery, Alabama in the 1950s. I still remember him saying: Walk, walk, walk. (Interview Elizabeth White, April, 1991).

Today the Shearer Cottage is still open to guests though the accommodation is structured into convenience apartments. The large dining room is no longer used to serve a family dinner for all of the guests, but the spirit of conviviality and community lives on.

Rev. Oscar Denniston

Bradley Memorial Church, 1907

In 1900, the Reverend Oscar Denniston came to Martha's Vineyard from Jamaica at the request of a white minister, Madison Edwards. The Reverend Edwards was then the minister of the Seamen's Bethel in Vineyard Haven. Oscar Denniston became a leader of the community of color on Martha's Vineyard which then numbered 175 people. At one point, he ran for the school committee but was unsuccessful. His son, Dean Denniston, in an interview with Linsey Lee, commented that people were shocked at the idea of a black man on the school committee. "Next thing we'll have black school teachers. Well we've lived to see a black superintendent." (*Vineyard Voices,* Linsey Lee 2004) The Reverend Denniston became involved with the Bradley Memorial Church and served as its pastor until 1946. The Bradley Memorial was named after Isabelle Bradley who provided citizenship and literacy classes for the Portuguese immigrants at the beginning of the 20th century. Reference to the Reverend Denniston can be found in the *Boston Guardian,* the

renowned African-American paper edited by William Munroe Trotter. The issue of August 7, 1933, includes a regular column, "Oak Bluffs Breezes" which refers to the illness of Reverend Denniston the "well-beloved pastor of the Bradley Memorial Church." The late Mr. Milton Jeffers of Edgartown remembered attending Reverend Denniston's church, and believed that it was the first black church on Martha's Vineyard. He described Reverend Denniston as "a very nice man, very tall and a wonderful preacher." (Interview, Milton Jeffers, 1991) The Denniston home is situated on Masonic Avenue in Oak Bluffs not far from the building on Dukes County Avenue that housed the Pentecostal church.

Site #11 — Bradley Memorial Church, Masonic Avenue, Oak Bluffs

Bradley Memorial Church

Miss Virginia Swann

Another interesting story is that of Miss Virginia Swann who many of our elder Island residents remember as a remarkable character. She lived for many years in Oak Bluffs before her tragic death during a house fire. She is recalled as a very small woman who because of an untreated childhood accident had significant physical disabilities, and yet successfully catered for social events and worked as a housekeeper.

Born in the South in the years of enslavement, it is not yet clear why she came to the Vineyard, but she carved a place for herself in the maritime culture of Oak Bluffs. During her years on the Island, she was famous as the woman who used to sit and watch the boats come in reliving memories known only to her. The records of the *Vineyard Gazette* show that upon her death, a local businessman paid for a headstone for her grave in the Oak Bluffs cemetery on Vineyard Avenue.

The Heritage Trail History Project intends to commemorate Miss Swan's life through a formal acknowledgment.

Circa 1900

The late Mr. Madison Denniston estimated that the year-round Martha's Vineyard community of the early 20th century included about 30 people of color. Among them were John Pollard, a Civil War veteran, who ran a dining room in the Highlands, and his sister in law, Mrs. Matthews. Mrs. Sarah Wentworth is mentioned as the mother of three sons, one of whom, Arthur, was the first African-American graduate of the Oak Bluffs High School. Other names mentioned were George Wormley who owned the gas station on New York Avenue in Oak Bluffs, and George Fry and his wife, Ella. George Fry was for many years a cobbler on Circuit Avenue in Oak Bluffs. The other names he mentioned were: Medie Wright and her sister Nelly Hooks, John Green, Amos Haskins, John Randolph, Virginia Swann, Mrs. Tilman, Mable Hughes and Mrs. Kibbie.

THE UNTOLD STORIES —
A VINEYARD SCRAPBOOK

1917

Images of Valor

From 1914 until 1918, Europe fought in the mud, tears and blood of trench warfare on the western front in France and Belgium. In the east the poorly equipped Russian army struggled to hold back German forces while sharing one gun among three soldiers. For three years, the soldiers lived in subhuman conditions, enduring water-filled trenches, poison gas, subzero temperatures and awaiting the order to leave their miserable sanctuary and dash across no-man's land toward the enemy trenches, a journey that very few would survive. By 1917, the casualties were enormous and the "war to end all wars" continued its daily monotonous horror with no clear indication of ending.

Into this horror came a new participant. The United States of America declared war on Germany in April of 1917, but did not send troops to France until the early fall of that year.

"Make way for democracy! We saved it in France, and by the Great Jehovah, we will save it in the United States of America, or know the reason why.

—W.E.B. Du Bois

100,000 AFRICAN-AMERICANS BARRED FROM FIGHTING WITH WHITE TROOPS JOIN WITH FRENCH

The delay was partly due to a shortage of adequately trained American soldiers. Many African-Americans enlisted in the military — 370,000 in all — but three quarters of them were relegated to labor battalions. Those 100,000 who did fight were segregated into separate units (the 369th and 372nd). They fought under French officers because they were not allowed to fight with American soldiers who were white. To the war-weary French, the color of the soldiers who fought with them was not an issue. The African-Americans were welcomed and honored for their bravery.

At a ceremony held in France to honor the contributions made by the United States soldiers of color, Jean-Luc Mathieu, a Frenchman whose grandfather died fighting alongside the African-American soldiers of the 369th New York regiment, observed: "I am grateful to those men for coming to our country to fight. We never think of them as black soldiers, just soldiers who were brave men."

During the victory parade in New York at the end of World War I, the African-American regiments who took part in the parade were "marching in the extraordinarily dramatic phalanx formation of the French Army. Shoulder to shoulder from curb to curb, they stretched in great massed squares, 35 feet wide by 35 feet long of men, helmets and bayonets. Through the newly erected Victory Arch at 25th and 5th Ave., they tramped far up the avenue in an endless mass of dark-skinned, grim faced, heavy-booted veterans of many a French battlefield" (Katz, *The Negro in American History*).

The bravery of these African-American soldiers was instrumental in holding the Germans at bay at dozens of battles including Chateau Thierry. The French government awarded the Croix de Guerre to these regiments while their own government was sadly silent.

EDWARD JANNIFER LIVED IN CAMBRIDGE, MA AND OAK BLUFFS

All stories that are played on the world's great stages have players whose names are rarely known, many of whom come from small communities. It is so with this story. An album of sepia photographs that told a family's story was given to Carrie Camillo Tankard, a board member of the African-American Heritage Trail. The donor did not know the family's name, but with a magnifying glass in hand we searched those photographs and a story unfolded.

Research has shown that the family's name was Jannifer and they had a home in Oak Bluffs and another in Cambridge. Amid the photographs of an idyllic Vineyard summer, we found the young soldier, whom we now know to be Edward Jannifer, dressed in the uniform of a United States soldier from World War I, proudly serving his country. Photographs show him as a cavalry soldier sitting on his horse with groups of soldiers posing around artillery.

AFRICAN-AMERICANS FOUGHT ALONGSIDE
FRENCH INFANTRYMEN

But the most interesting photograph shows Edward Jannifer and three other United States soldiers of color posing for a group photograph with a large number of white soldiers in different uniforms. This exciting discovery was steamed off the page and revealed the writing "France, 1918" on the back. The white soldiers are French, and the Heritage Trail has in its possession another piece of the previously lost — or forgotten — history of African-Americans in the United States. The photograph shows the camaraderie that existed between the African-American soldiers and the French infantrymen who fought alongside them.

THE BATTLE FOR EQUALITY AT HOME
WAS STILL TO BE WON

Mr. Jannifer, formerly of Oak Bluffs, was among those African-Americans who so desired to fight for his country he joined in combat with the army of an ally when his own nation would not have him take up arms. The democracy he helped save in Europe was yet incomplete at home. These African-Americans served their country gallantly, earned the gratitude of the French people and proved their own valor in the trying conditions of horror of World War I. In 1919, they returned to a country where the battle for true equality had still to be won.

We return

We return from fighting.

We return fighting.

"Make way for democracy! We saved it in France, and by the Great Jehovah, we will save it in the United States of America, or know the reason why" (W.E.B. Du Bois, "Returning Soldiers," *Crisis,* May 1919).

I am grateful to those men for coming to our country to fight. We never think of them as black soldiers, just soldiers who were brave men.

Jean-Luc Mathieu

Miss Louisa Izett

THE LANDLADIES OF OAK BLUFFS

1890s-1930s
Dedicated: 2000

Women who dared

Written in collaboration with Carrie Camillo Tankard

Property restrictions existed on the Island, and deeds for certain parcels in the Highlands area of Oak Bluffs included the wording: "this property is to be occupied by people of the white race and the Christian religion except in the capacity of servants." There were also restrictions on the Camp Ground area. A woman of color identified as Mrs. Smith, was a proprietor of an Oak Bluffs guesthouse. Shortly after she bought a nearby cottage in the Campground from her former employer, she was forced to give up her home and move to Circuit Avenue.

An article in the *Martha's Vineyard Herald* of July 13, 1889, stated that "Mr. Matthews, a Selectmen, said and did nothing, but as a private citizen he naturally objected to having a

The Landladies of Oak Bluffs: because of them, people of color were able to live, work, and vacation here.

Louisa Izett: This house was established in 1899 by Louisa Izett — an entrepreneur who dared — as a guest house for African-American people.

*Site #7 — Landladies
Site #8 — Izett House*

91

colored lodging house next door to him. Mr. Eldridge did the liberal thing....secured her another house in which she is comfortably settled and more satisfied with than the other in the Camp Ground."

MISS IZETT AND MRS. O'BRIEN BOUGHT 121 LOWER CIRCUIT AVENUE

During the same era, Miss Louisa Izett bought a property that is now 121 Lower Circuit Avenue, and the adjacent property, currently the Tivoli Inn. Together with her sister, Mrs. Georgia O'Brien, Miss Izett opened two guesthouses that catered to people of color. Some of their guests were seasonal workers in Edgartown, and some were vacationers in Oak Bluffs.

The present owner of 121 Lower Circuit Avenue is Mrs. Ora McFarlane. Her husband Stanley, was the nephew of Miss Izett and Mrs. O'Brien. Mrs. McFarlane remembers that her husband's aunts were among the women of color who were responsible for establishing a successful black presence on the Vineyard.

> *They made it possible for African-American people to live and work on Martha's Vineyard. They helped so many young black people have a home here. It was seven dollars a week for room and board, but if it happened that the person only had five they would take that because they knew that it was not easy to make enough money. They*

Mrs. Georgia O'Brien

were very ambitious entrepreneurs, but they cared about the people who stayed with them. Aunt Georgia's house [now the Tivoli Inn] was the one where people would socialize and have parties. People of color had to make their own entertainment because they were not welcome in the restaurants and hotels. They used to have card parties and dances and famous people, like Adam Clayton Powell, would regularly attend them (Ora McFarlane, September, 2000).

1930s BRING OPPORTUNITIES FOR ENTERPRISING WOMEN OF COLOR

During the years of the Depression, following the collapse of Wall Street in 1929, many owners of summer homes on the Vineyard were forced to sell. When houses became available in the Hiawatha Park area of Lower Circuit Avenue in Oak Bluffs, African-Americans bought and renovated many. The financial collapse caused house prices to plummet, and this created an opportunity for enterprising women of color. Sustained by their dreams of financial independence, these African-American woman opened boarding houses that allowed people of color to become part of the Vineyard community.

CARRIE "AUNT CASH" ANDERSON: These enterprising women included Carrie "Aunt Cash" Anderson whose husband was a tailor in Boston. She operated a business pressing clothes until she realized her ambition to buy a property on Hiawatha Park that she converted into a boarding house. Her next door neighbor, Carrie Tappin, operated a laundry business and a boarding house. Neighbors recollect Mrs. Tappin collecting and delivering laundry on a little red wagon while in her kitchen numerous flat irons awaited use (Interview Marianne Bradley, 2000).

MRS. GLADYS BRIGGS' MOTHER: A little further down on Pocasset Avenue Mrs. Gladys Briggs still operates a small hotel, a property her mother bought while employed as a domestic servant by the Penny family. Mrs. Briggs recollects that her childhood in Oak Bluffs was a very happy one. "The Island is a very friendly place. When I was a child here, our next door neighbor Mrs. Amaral would always send over a couple of pies to my mother when we had company. She thought nothing of it" (Interview, Gladys Briggs, 2000).

MRS. LOUISE B. JACKSON: Mrs. Louise B. Jackson lived on nearby Nashawena Park. She too opened her house to guests, and her granddaughter, E. Jacqueline Hunt, recalls that there was always room for one more at her grandmother's table. Jacqueline Hunt later became president of the Vineyard's chapter of the NAACP.

ELIZABETH LEWIS BEARD: On Warwick Avenue, Elizabeth Lewis Beard and her daughters Elsie and Ethel, operated the

Lewis Dining Room. Their business was enormously successful. Their business cards read: "After the dance and any time — always open." (Interview, Stephen Lewis, 2000)

Many landladies along South Circuit Avenue and the surrounding areas were responsible for the area's economic vitality. One such was Mrs. Rudene Hopkins whose children and grandchildren – the Randolph family – still live on Martha's Vineyard.

The Heritage Trail dedicated two sites to the memory of the entrepreneurial landladies in October, 2000. A plaque on the property at 121 South Circuit Avenue honors Miss Izett, and one on a bench in Hiawatha Park, commemorates all of the landladies for their remarkable achievements.

Lilllian Garcia and her sister Ora McFarlane, who now owns the Izett house.

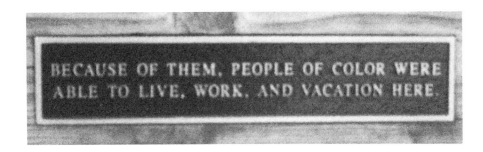

THE BUNNY COTTAGE

1937-1945

Isabel Washington Powell 1908-2007
Adam Clayton Powell 1908-1972

Isabel Powell and Congressman Adam Clayton Powell Jr.

"Keep the Faith Baby"

A huge crowd gathered on August 24, 2003 to celebrate the dedication of the home of Isabel Powell as a site on the Heritage Trail. Her house, on the corner of Dorothy West and Myrtle Avenues, is the home that she bought with Congressman Adam Clayton Powell during their marriage. Mrs. Powell is considered the matriarch of the African-American summer community.

She began her career as a dancer and actress in Harlem. Prior to her marriage to Congressman Powell in 1933, Isabel appeared at the famed Cotton Club in Harlem, New York, and

Site #12 — The Powell House

AFRICAN AMERICAN HERITAG

THE POW

"KEEP THE
ADAM

THIS, THE SUMMER HOME OF ADAM CLAYTON POWELL,
FROM 1937 TO THE PRESENT, HAS BEEN A POPULAR

ADAM CLAYTON POWELL REPRESENTED THE HARLEM (
1945-70. HE WAS THE FIRST AFRICAN AMERICAN ELEC
AS CHAIRMAN OF THE HOUSE EDUCATION AND LABOR
OF CIVIL RIGHTS LEGISLATION DURING THE KENNI
LEGISLATIVE RECORD ENDING WITH: "I LOVE AMERICA
OF SOCIAL JUSTICE TO AMERICAN LIFE. HE WAS ALSO
3,000 MEMBER ABYSSINIAN BAPTIST CHURCH IN HARLE
OF HIS CHURCH MEMBERS TO THE ISLAND.

ISABEL POWELL WAS AN ACTRESS AND SINGER APPEA
AND EARLY 1930'S. SHE WAS A LEAD DANCER AT T
AS A SPECIAL EDUCATION TEACHER IN THE NEW Y

SINCE 1945, ISABEL POWELL HAS SPENT EVERY SUM
ENTERTAINING THEM WITH HER "BLOODY MARYS" AND
AND CO-DISCOVERER OF THE NORTH POLE IN 1909,

ADAM CLAYTON POWELL LOVED MARTHA'S VINEYARD
HIS CIVIC AND COMMUNITY BUILDING SKILLS ON TI

THE HERITAGE TRAIL HONORS AND RI
WORK IN TRANSFORMING SOCIAL JUST
HER CONTRIBUTIONS TO THE CULT
VINEYARD.

AUGU

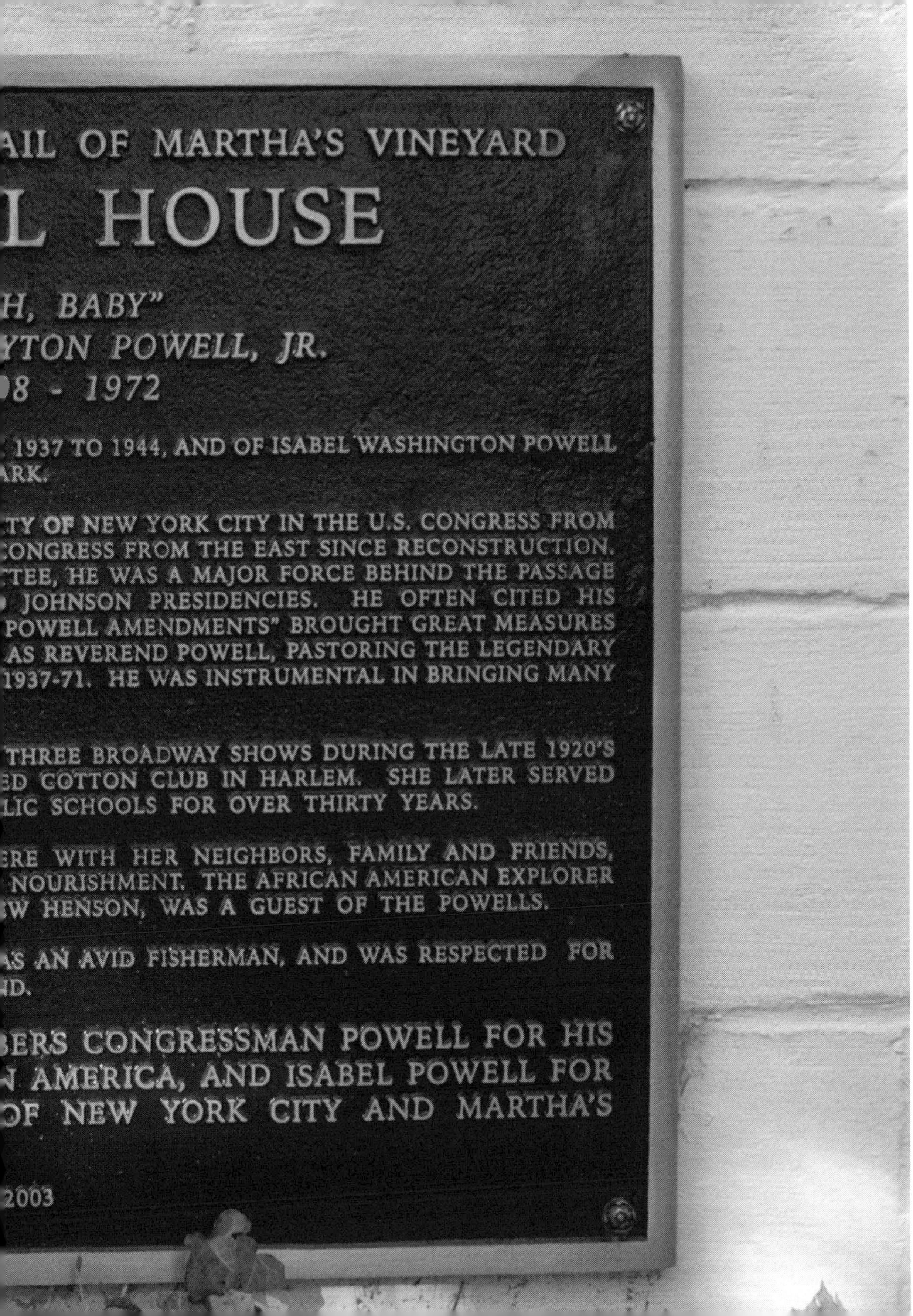

AIL OF MARTHA'S VINEYARD

L HOUSE

H, BABY"
YTON POWELL, JR.
8 - 1972

1937 TO 1944, AND OF ISABEL WASHINGTON POWELL
ARK.

TY OF NEW YORK CITY IN THE U.S. CONGRESS FROM
CONGRESS FROM THE EAST SINCE RECONSTRUCTION.
TEE, HE WAS A MAJOR FORCE BEHIND THE PASSAGE
JOHNSON PRESIDENCIES.   HE OFTEN CITED HIS
POWELL AMENDMENTS" BROUGHT GREAT MEASURES
AS REVEREND POWELL, PASTORING THE LEGENDARY
1937-71. HE WAS INSTRUMENTAL IN BRINGING MANY

THREE BROADWAY SHOWS DURING THE LATE 1920'S
ED COTTON CLUB IN HARLEM. SHE LATER SERVED
LIC SCHOOLS FOR OVER THIRTY YEARS.

ERE WITH HER NEIGHBORS, FAMILY AND FRIENDS,
NOURISHMENT. THE AFRICAN AMERICAN EXPLORER
W HENSON, WAS A GUEST OF THE POWELLS.

AS AN AVID FISHERMAN, AND WAS RESPECTED FOR
D.

BERS CONGRESSMAN POWELL FOR HIS
AMERICA, AND ISABEL POWELL FOR
OF NEW YORK CITY AND MARTHA'S

2003

starred in a Broadway musical entitled *Harlem.* At the time of their marriage, Adam Clayton Powell was a junior minister at the Abyssinian Baptist Church in Harlem. Isabel Powell retired from show business after her marriage to please her husband's family, and for the years of their marriage, she was the supportive wife of the minister of New York's most famous black church. In his autobiography, Clayton Powell referred to Isabel as the "most beautiful woman I have ever seen."

THE POWELLS BUY IN OAK BLUFFS HIGHLANDS

The Powells bought the Highlands home in 1937, and gave it the nickname Bunny Cottage. During the years the couple lived there together, they entertained illustrious guests such as Matthew Henson, the African-American who explored the North Pole.

Adam Clayton Powell loved the Vineyard, and especially enjoyed fishing. He wrote a newspaper column appealing to "his black brothers and sisters" to come to the Vineyard. He was a charismatic personality remembered by many for his charm and his determination to achieve racial justice. In 1989, the late Elizabeth White shared a story with me relating to the famous Congressman.

Adam looked white, and he was very affable and charming. One day he was standing in the doorway of one of the Oak Bluffs businesses chatting with the owner. The man said to Adam

"look at all these colored people on Circuit Avenue. They are taking over. Its terrible." Adam smiled and walked out of there, and organized a boycott that went on for years (Interview, Elizabeth White, 1989). Doris Jackson, of the Shearer Cottage concurs: "Adam looked white, but he always thought black."

Isabel and Adam Clayton Powell divorced in 1945, but the Bunny Cottage remains very unchanged. Mrs. Powell lived in the house after the divorce, and has continued her famous tradition of entertainment until the present day. At her request, the Heritage Trail plaque on her house refers to the amazing Bloody Marys she makes for her guests. She still cherishes all the keepsakes of her life with Clayton Powell including his fishing rods. The house in many ways seems like a museum of their life together. Following the divorce, Isabel Powell became a special education teacher in New York City for 30 years.

POWELL IS HARLEM'S CONGRESSMAN
FROM 1945-1971

Congressman Powell's career is well known. As the charismatic and effective leader of the Education and Labor Committee in U.S. House of Representatives during the years of the Kennedy and Johnson administrations, Powell was responsible for an impressive series of civil rights laws. His most famous contribution is the Powell Amendment which

Remembering Rev. Powell

Congressman Powell is remembered fondly by Heather Rynd of West Tisbury. During Heather's childhood, her mother, Valerie Lethbridge Rynd, was the Congressman's confidante, and he is remembered as a friendly and kind person who taught Heather to say her prayers. "I have never forgotten the prayers he taught me when I was so little. I think that memory and the one of hearing him preach at the Abyssinian Baptist Church in Harlem during the 1960s are the most vivid recollections I have of him. He had a powerful spirituality that was mesmerizing."

Valerie Lethbridge Rynd met Adam Clayton Powell at Dune Deck in the Hamptons in the early 1950s. Because of her friendship with the Congressman, Lethbridge Rynd was ostracized by the beach club communities of the Hamptons, and as a result, the organization canceled all of her family memberships in the beach clubs. "Those beach clubs were very bigoted. They did not allow Jews or black people or anyone who was not one of their own little ethnic clique. My mother hated that kind of prejudice." The relationship ended, but Heather Rynd remembers going to hear Reverend Powell preach at the Abyssian Baptist Church in the 1960s. She recounts vivid memories of visiting him in the hospital when he was terminally ill. (Interview, Heather Rynd, 2004)

forbids racial and gender discrimination in all federally funded projects.

The dedication of the Bunny Cottage as a formal site on the Heritage Trail was celebrated by politicians, police chiefs and public administrators as well as Mrs. Powell's many friends and neighbors. Though physically frail, Isabel Powell has an indomitable spirit. She addressed the crowd at the dedication:

> *I am a human being, and I love all kinds of people because I believe that we are all just human beings, and there is no need for difference between us. I have had a wonderful life, and I have had all kinds of friends. Life is precious and it should be enjoyed. (Isabel Powell, 2000).*

HERITAGE PLAQUE HONORS THE LIVES OF ISABEL AND ADAM CLAYTON POWELL

The plaque on the Powell House describes the life achievements of Isabel and Adam Clayton Powell, and underscored the role each played in the history of African-American people in the 20th century. The inscription includes the admonition, "keep the faith baby," the parting words for which Adam Clayton Powell was famous. Isabel Powell still spends each summer in Oak Bluffs entertaining friends, guests and all those who stop at the house to read the plaque.

Joe Overton

THE OVERTON HOUSE

1960s

Joe Overton never forgot how hard it was for black folks

The Heritage Trail dedicated its 17th site on September 5, 2004 with the induction of the Vila Rosa, on Narragansett Avenue in Oak Bluffs. Formerly the property of the Overton family, the home was declared the "Summer White House" of the African-American people during the years of the Civil Rights movement. Prominent among the guests who stayed in this elegant residence were Dr. Martin Luther King Jr., Bayard Rustin, J. Philip Randolph, Jesse Jackson and C. B. Powell. Their hosts were the Overton family of New York and Oak Bluffs.

Summer White for the Civil Rights Movement: a house of love and tranquility, it provided solace and inspiration for those who worked tirelessly for justice and freedom

JOE OVERTON WORKED FOR ECONOMIC JUSTICE

Joseph Overton was a union organizer and political leader who worked for civil rights and economic development for African-American communities during the years when people of color were challenging the nation for inclusion

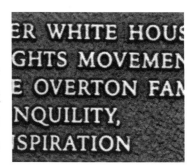

Site #15 — The Overton House

in the American dream. The focus of his activism was economic injustice. As a union organizer and leading member of the NAACP, he challenged the prevailing power structure effectively and often. Neighbor and friend, Mildred Henderson, remembers him as being a strong advocate for economic advancement for people of color. "He never forgot how hard it was for black people to get ahead, and I remember him urging everyone to buy the brownstones between 145th and 181st streets in Harlem. He really wanted to help build the confidence of black people" (Interview, Mildred Henderson, 2004).

Newspaper articles found in the house tell a story of a man who fought to open youth centers in Harlem, and who led demonstrations and strikes against economic discrimination. Mildred Henderson comments that Joe Overton grew into his role as a leader of African-American people. "When we first knew him, he was unsophisticated. He was always a good man, a sweet man, a great speaker, but over the years he became very polished and skilled. He never forgot his roots no matter how many famous people he knew."

OVERTON BECAME CHARISMATIC POLITICAL FIGURE

Ms. Henderson and her sister, Ruth Scorville Bonaparte, remember that Joe Overton was very friendly with C. B. Powell, the owner of the *Amsterdam News* and J. Philip Randolph, the leader of the Pullman Porters Union. "Mr. Powell lived down the road, and he was always at the Overton house as was J. Philip Randolph. I think that they had a great influence on him. They were activists and friends, and both Powell and Randolph were men of great influence" (Interview, Ruth Scorville Bonaparte, 2004).

The sisters recalled that their family and the Overtons bought their houses on Naragansett Avenue in Oak Bluffs in 1956. "We were the first three black families on the street, and so we knew each other very well. It's never easy being the first anything, but we supported each other, and some of the other neighbors made us welcome" (Interview Ruth Bonaparte Scorville, 2004).

Those around him recall Joe Overton as a charismatic political figure who knew everyone and was absorbed in his political life in New York City. Photographs found in the Vila Rosa show him with many significant African-American

THIS HOUSE SERVED AS THE SUMMER WHITE HOUSE FOR THE LEADERS OF THE CIVIL RIGHTS MOVEMENT WHO STAYED HERE AS GUESTS OF THE OVERTON FAMILY. A HOUSE OF LOVE AND TRANQUILITY, IT PROVIDED SOLACE AND INSPIRATION FOR THOSE WHO WORKED TIRELESSLY FOR JUSTICE AND FREEDOM. GUESTS INCLUDED: DR. MARTIN LUTHER KING, MALCOLM X, ADAM CLAYTON POWELL, JR., JOE LOUIS, HARRY BELEFONTE

VILLA ROSA OWNED BY THE ZILA FAMILY. 2004

community leaders. In one memorable photo he is posed with Fidel Castro at the Hotel Theresa in Harlem. Mildred Henderson recalls that he was a hard-working man who made up for his absences with extravagant gifts. "He would come in on the 'daddy boat' on Friday night, and we were all so jealous of the gifts that he brought for his kids. There would be bikes and toys. We used to think of him as being like Santa" (Interview, Mildred Henderson, 2004).

TRADITIONAL CULTURAL IDEAS PREVAILED

The Overton family attended the now defunct Pentecostal church on Dukes County Avenue, and the sisters recollect Gloria Overton "marching her children to church every Sunday." The picture that friends and neighbors draw of the

Joe Overton and friends with Fidel Castro at the Hotel Theresa in Harlem.

Overton summer home is one where the famous visited, but where traditional cultural ideas prevailed. Mildred Henderson remembers that the Overton family had relatives in Baltimore who used to bring soft-shell crabs which everyone shared at beach picnics.

Among the famous guests was Dr. Martin Luther King, Jr: "I remember Dr. King sitting on the Overton's porch reading, writing and discussing. He used to love the beach, but we never bothered him. We gave him space, and he never seemed to be asking for anything special" (Interview Ruth Bonaparte Scorville, 2004). Words from Dr. King's final speech are included on the Heritage Trail plaque:

> I've seen the promised land. I may not get there with you, but I want you to know that we, as a people, will get to the promised land and I am happy tonight. I am not worried about anything.

The Heritage Trail chose to honor the Overton house because its existence provides a tangible link with a confident and successful community leader whose contributions were largely unrecorded. In this house on Naragansett Avenue in Oak Bluffs, a new vision of America was crafted. In the words of Jerry Jacobs who unveiled the plaque. "Joe was someone who cared. He used to sit at that kitchen table, and try to urge us to make plans for our future, and to succeed. I was only a kid then, but I knew that he wanted every young brother and sister to be successful in a better world."

"I've seen the promised land. I may not get there with you, but I want you to know that we, as a people, will get to the promised land and I am happy tonight. I am not worried about anything."

—Martin Luther King, Jr.

SENATOR EDWARD BROOKE

U.S. Senate: 1967-1979

We have much to be proud of, and much to share

The former home of Senator Edward Brooke on Nashawena Avenue in Oak Bluffs was dedicated as a site on the Heritage Trail in October of 2003. Senator Brooke was the first African-American member of the U.S. Senate since Reconstruction.

When the Commonwealth of Massachusetts appointed him to the office of attorney general, he became the first African-American to hold that office.

Those attending the dedication recognized the remarkable achievements of Senator Brooke and acknowledged the racism he endured while breaking those barriers. Brooke indeed withstood dual pressures. At the same time that he had to perform in the world of power and privilege, he was aware that his life would be the role model for a generation of young African-American people.

Edward Brooke purchased this property in 1958. He named it the Island Club. His purpose was to establish a club that black people could call their own, since most of the private clubs on the Island were segregated.

Site #14—former home of Senator Edward Brooke

SENATOR BROOKE'S ACHIEVEMENTS
INSPIRE OTHER AFRICAN-AMERICANS

Senator Brooke's home was a social center of African-Americans of influence and education who created their own summer community at a time of racial separation. Peggy Amos, the Senator's niece observed that "historically, restrictions were placed on people of color, but in this world, no restrictions or limitations were recognized or accepted." During a session of shared reflection, Betty Dixon, a summer resident, remarked: "people of color have been here for hundreds of years, but until the Heritage Trail began its work, it seemed like no one even knew that we were here."

Speaking on behalf of the Senator, Peggy Amos delivered a message that prioritized his lifetime commitments. "People need to know their history and African-American history should take its place with all the other stories. "We have much to be proud of and much to share. History is the means by which we can do that. We must be sure that we teach it, and that we learn it" (Senator Edward Brooke, 2003).

The Senator's great-nephew, David Amos, paid tribute to his achievements:

> *All my life I have heard about Senator Brooke's accomplishments. I have seen the limousines, and the Courthouse in Boston named after him. I have traveled with him, and seen the bodyguard. I look at that and I see what is possible for a*

black man. Its very unusual to see a black man in that position, and it makes me believe that someday I could be like him. That's why its so important for me and for other black kids to understand that we have to work hard in school and struggle because there is a point to it. We can be somebody (David Amos, 2003).

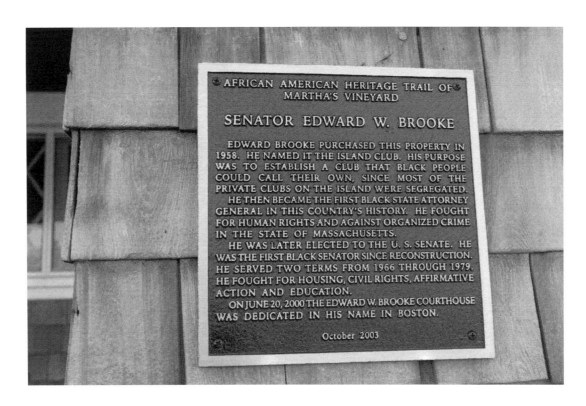

Martha's Vineyard African American Heritage Trail

Guinea

Rebecca Amos was brought to America from Guinea, Africa as a slave. She is seen here with her daughter, Nancy, who was later thought of as a witch. Nancy, or "Black Nance," as she was called, would bless or curse sailors going out to sea. Her son, William A. Martin, was the first African American whaling captain. All are a part of the Martha's Vineyard African American Heritage Trail.

Vineyard Gazette
January 2, 1857

Mrs. Nancy Michael known to most of our readers by the familiar cognomen of "Black Nance" is no more. She departed this life on Saturday last, at a very advanced age. Probably she was not far from 100 years old. She had changed but little in her appearance for some years past, and those who knew her 50 years ago looked upon her as an old woman.

She was very remarkable character in her day. Naturally possessing a real feeling, she was fond of children and showed anxiety to their sickness, and there are not few among us who have not at some time been indebted to her. Possessed of a strong natural mind, she acquired great influence over some of our people—not only those who are cast under the eye of...

MARTHA'S VINEYARD REGIONAL HIGH SCHOOL

1999

People like us don't get our names on plaques

In June, 1999, the Heritage Trail History Project dedicated the Martha's Vineyard Regional High School as a site on the Heritage Trail. A plaque in the main foyer honors the achievements of the school basketball teams in the early 1970s.

CHAMPION TEAM IS HONORED

The suggestion for this plaque had come from the Island community, and its installation generated both interest and controversy. The then school principal, Dr. Gregory Scotten, enthusiastically supported the notion of honoring teams that had brought distinction to the school, particularly since the players represented the Vineyard's diverse ethnic communities.

Some suggested that the appropriate place for the plaque would be the in the school's athletic area. But only the athletes use this area of the school building, and such a distant

This plaque salutes the remarkable achievements of the MVRHS boys' basketball teams for the years 1971-1974 and the girls' basketball team of 1974-1975. These teams reflect the diversity of our Island. They were drawn from the African-American, Native American, Cape Verdean, Portuguese and Anglo communities

Site #16 — MVRHS

placement was not acceptable to the board of the Heritage Trail History Project.

The board felt that the plaque should be displayed in the main entrance hall of the school in a place of distinction among the school's many honors where it could be seen by everyone who entered the building. The most important consideration was the prominent placement of the various Vineyard family names whose accomplishments and histories would never again fade from memory. In this way, two of the important aspects of the Heritage Trail mission could be realized: restoring lost histories and recording the undocumented achievements of our community.

Amaury Bannister and Ronald Brown, two African-American former students who had played with great distinction for the team, dedicated the plaque. At the reception following the dedication, one of the former athletes whose name is inscribed spoke briefly. "This plaque means a lot to me. All of our names are on it, and we are not the kind of people who get our names on plaques. I will never forget this" (Lester Baptiste, June, 1999).

STUDENTS CREATE MURALS OF LOCAL AFRICAN-AMERICAN HISTORY

In the years that followed, the high school has become the site of four murals that depict scenes from the African American history of Martha's Vineyard. These remarkable works of art were painted by students as part of their connection with the Heritage Trail History Project which sponsors an annual exhibition of student art work and research projects.

A moving painting of Nancy Michael, the woman of power, painted by Joe Murphy in 1999 reminds us of her unusual influence across the arc of her life. The mural shows Nancy as an old woman looking back on her life, depicts her as a young girl being sold away from her mother, portrays her as a nurse to the children of the privileged and prosperous in Edgartown and suggests her as a mysterious woman of power haunting the

Edgartown waterfront. Another interesting mural painted by Bronwyn Burns in 2000 honors Captain William A. Martin. He stands on his ship in a contemplative mood against a background of a dark blue, star-studded sky.

In 2002, Brooke Emin and Lauraye White painted a large mural depicting the Island of Martha's Vineyard that identifies the sites of the Heritage Trail. In 2003, Lily Morris and Elyse Fortes finished a remarkable mural that represents Nancy Michael as a young child with her mother, Rebecca, the woman from Africa. In this painting, both Rebecca and Nancy are veiled in the Islamic manner. The mural includes a map of Guinea in Africa, and a complete copy of the obituary that appeared in the *Vineyard Gazette* after Nancy Michael died.

All of these murals are more than decorative pieces of art. Each is a dramatic interpretation of African-American life in the 18th and 19th centuries on Martha's Vineyard. Each one tells a specific story with historical accuracy and empathy. They are testaments to how much the students of the Regional High School have involved themselves with the Heritage Trail History Project, and what such dedication has meant to them as the poem "Rebecca's Eyes" conveys:

Briana Valenti, a student who was involved with the Trail, commented:

> *I will never forget the Heritage Trail. Its just so valid to the Island. It helps African Americans kids to see themselves differently and it helps*

Rebecca's Eyes

Stolen from my home
moved to this new place
My life is harder than it was
I can feel it in my face
A face of hope and sadness
A face that's seen too much
Looking for someone to save me
Knowing I can not save myself
Never shall my eyes grow cold
For I know home is near to my heart

Oh, Indian man
Man who knows and loves me
Indian man whose face holds my comfort
Man that saved me
Keep me safe in this foreign place
Sometimes I hope for a way out, a better life
A way back to Africa
I hope for my children to do better
I hope that no one else is stolen
from home

Always wanting! Hate my Master!
Need a trail to lead me out of darkness
I can not stand this place
Guinea is where I long to stand

By Gaby Leon Guerrero
and Sarah LaPiana,
Sophomore class, 2002.

white kids to see things differently too. Its so important to know about that. I would not have done the research myself, but I think we will all need to know that information in the future. I have been on the Trail three times I have great memories of seeing students perched on the Rock, and eating soul food at Lola's and when you have memories like that you have really learned something. I would love to see more Trails developed for the Portuguese, the Irish and for all of us (Weintraub, Lost Histories and Lost Heroes: The African American Heritage Trail of Martha's Vineyard, 2000).

Brian Scott, a student who served on the board of the Heritage Trail History Project, reflected on the success of the project with students.

I think the History Project should develop its work in the school. In a few years, it has gone from just reading about it to having sites all over the Island. I like the way students work on it now: looking after sites, painting murals, writing poetry, singing to honor it – all kinds of ways. The annual tour of the Trail is very popular with students. Keep that involvement going and make it deeper.

Before I worked on the Trail project, all I learned about African-American history, all I heard

Jade Cash, Peg Regan and Brian Scott at Heritage Trail Awards Ceremony.

Students enjoy soul-food lunch at Lola's restaurant as part of Heritage Trail tour.

about, was slave ships, and that is just another world, just not real. But the Heritage Trail project makes you understand that it really did happen here.

For the students, it is too early in their lives to appreciate it because they are not yet developed into a situation that they can completely understand, but later they will and they will be able to educate other people about the African-American history of this Island. We, students of color, will say that we are really appreciated and I think that this gives us more respect for ourselves on the island. (Weintraub, *Lost Histories and Lost Heroes: The African American Heritage Trail of Martha's Vineyard*, 2000)

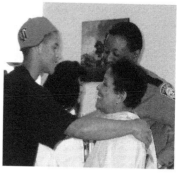

Jade Cash, Carrie Camillo Tankard and police chief Joseph Carter at awards ceremony.

African American Heritage Trail

Trail

Gospel Tabernacle

Home of Dorothy West

The Grace Church

The Shearer Cottage

Eastville Cemetery

Powell House

The plaque of Rebecca

The Martha's Vineyard Regional High School

The Seaport of Menemsha

Pulpit Rock

To Wampanoug Tribe

'MARCH 2002'

ALL AROUND THE TOWN,
THE STORIES ABOUND

A rich tradition of African-American participation in the community in this area of Oak Bluffs remains today, a testament to a tradition of religious worship, civic action and social conscience. An organization of African-American women who own homes in Oak Bluffs was formed in 1956. They have successfully raised funds for the Martha's Vineyard hospital, the NAACP, the Oak Bluffs library and many other community projects. During the 1960s, the organization purchased the Old Town Hall in Oak Bluffs and renamed it Cottagers Corner. Over the years, the Cottagers have provided activities for children and adolescents during the summer. We plan to dedicate the Cottagers building as a site on the Heritage Trail in 2006 in celebration of their 50th anniversary.

WE HOPE TO RESTORE THE PENTECOSTAL CHURCH

There are several other projects of immediate interest to the Heritage Trail History Project. We hope to acquire and restore the now defunct Pentecostal Church on Dukes County Avenue in Oak Bluffs. This small building played an important

Penetcostal Church
Dukes County Avenue
Oak Bluffs

role in the religious and community life of people of color on Martha's Vineyard. Though the building is in an advanced state of disrepair, traces are still evident that this was, indeed, a place of worship and spirituality. The board intends to continue its program of active advocacy to save the Captain Martin house on Chappaquiddick. This building, which was home to the Island's only African-American whaling captain, is an integral part of our community history. The History Project board has been vigilant in advocacy and education with regard to the Martin homestead. Our goal is to ensure that this vital link with our maritime past will not be lost.

WE ARE GATHERING ORAL HISTORY

Another goal of the Heritage Trail History Project is to continue the gathering of oral histories, the first volume of which was published in 2000, *Telling it Like It Is ... or Was*. Students interview members of our Island community to save their stories from extinction. From these interviews students learn significant information. In his interview with Christine Chambers, T.M. Araujo spoke of growing up in Tisbury.

> *He says that people were very prejudiced against people of color, and that every day he and his brothers and sisters would get chased home by the white kids. His father used to wait on the corner with a big strap and so if T.M. and his brothers would not fight the white kids who were tormenting them, they got a beating from their*

father. He says that it was like being between a rock and a hard place, but that the beating from his father was worse than anything he and his brothers got from the white kids. For that reason, they would stand and fight rather than get the beating (Christine Chambers interview T.M. Araujo in *Telling It Like It Is... Or Was,* 2000).

THE TRAIL PROJECT CONTINUES

The work of the Heritage Trail History Project will continue. There are more sites to be dedicated and much research is yet to be done. The program of education continues its refinement as it develops with each class of students. Every project, poem, investigation and insight from each student brings something new and valuable. The tour program in the summers will provide students with opportunities to act as educators for visitors.

WE ARE CONNECTING WITH NANTUCKET'S BLACK HERITAGE TRAIL

Connections have been made between the Heritage Trail History Project, and the Black Heritage Trail on Nantucket, and an annual exchange program has begun where students from the Vineyard travel to Nantucket to educate that community about the Vineyard's African-American history. Nantucket students travel to the Vineyard to reciprocate the effort.

The Trail itself is a physical entity providing visitors with a graphic reminder that the people whose lives are celebrated at these sites existed, and that their story is part of all of our stories. The work will continue, and more stories and artifacts will be added.

WE ARE WORKING TO PRESERVE OUR HERITAGE

This community history includes tragedy and amazing triumphs. During the summer months, Martha's Vineyard is home to many distinguished African-Americans who have achieved fame and material success. The guest list for the Shearer Cottage is like a roll call for famous community leaders and artists. The Overton house entertained guests who helped rewrite the history of the 20th century. Labor union organizers, civil rights activists and leaders such as Dr. Martin Luther King Jr. were among the visitors. There is a copy of a letter written by Dr. King in the archives of the *Vineyard Gazette*. In it, he apologizes for not being available to be interviewed by the paper during the summer of 1961.

> *I hope it will be possible for me to meet you at some other time. I am deeply grateful for all your encouraging words concerning the struggle in the south, and for the support that you gave the Montgomery Improvement Association* (Martin Luther King, Jr. September 17, 1961).

Martha's Vineyard has been home to a distinguished

whaling captain of African ancestry and three generations of his family stretching back to Rebecca, the woman from Africa. Here on this small Island, a group of entrepreneurial women of color opened their homes and made it possible for African American people to become part of this maritime community.

We are enriched by an inclusive Island history that records and celebrates the experiences of all communities. In this interdependent world, all stories have equal value, and we are all deprived when only some are told. The people of this Island have a shared heritage based in common struggles, shared skills and family connections. History is the story of the struggles, joys and cultural values that give meaning to all of our daily lives. It is the means by which we can examine what binds us together, and recognize the diverse nature of our community. This is the story of the African-American people of Martha's Vineyard, and of the building of the Heritage Trail that honored that story.

The African American Heritage Trail Continues to Grow: 10 New Sites

It has been ten years since the first edition of this book was published and those years have been busy and productive. Relationships have been built throughout the Island community and the Trail has become a well-known attraction for summer visitors and academic institutions.

The educational program at the Martha's Vineyard Regional High School has been developed into an annual exhibition, and the original goal of making sure that this history would never again be lost has been met.

Since 2005, ten more sites have been included in the Trail and a comprehensive story of African-American people on Martha's Vineyard has been recognized.

- The Cottagers' Corner building on Pequot Avenue in Oak Bluffs was dedicated as a site on the Trail honoring the hard work and community involvement of the 100 women who form that organization.

- The story of Barber Hammond, the first black entrepreneur in Vineyard Haven has been celebrated with a plaque on the building where he first opened his barber shop.

- The stories of the first people of color to be appointed to the school system have been saved for posterity and a plaque honoring their achievement placed on the school superintendent's building in Vineyard Haven.

- The first teacher of color at the Island's regional high school has been recognized as part of the story with a plaque honoring his sometimes challenging tenure.

- The five brave women from West Tisbury who traveled south in 1964 to help the struggle for justice and equality are now included on the Heritage Trail with a site honoring them in the town.

- The founding of the Vineyard chapter of the NAACP has been recognized and a moving ceremony held at St. Andrew's church in Edgartown.

- The former home of Harlem Renaissance writer, Dorothy West, has been dedicated as a site.

- In 2012, the home of Carrie and George Tankard in Oak Bluffs was dedicated as site #24 on the Heritage Trail honoring their lifelong commitment to civil rights and social justice.

- In 2013, Coleman's Corner was dedicated as site #25 honoring the achievements of Ralf Meshack Coleman known as the Dean of Boston's Black Theater and the family's long standing contribution to the Island.

- In June, 2015, the former home of Emma Chambers Maitland was dedicated as a site on the Trail honoring her remarkable life and achievements.

The Trail is a physical reminder of the stories of the people of this community. It is, and will continue to be, a celebration of lives lived with dignity, courage and creativity.

THE COTTAGERS CORNER

Pequot Avenue, Oak Bluffs

1956
Dedicated 2006

*"Success is liking yourself, liking what you do,
and liking how you do it."*

– Maya Angelou

*A volunteer
organization of
African-American
women created to
enhance the quality
of life on Martha's
Vineyard in the spirit
of fellowship and
community.*

Site #18 — Cottagers Corner

On July 5th, 2006 the Cottagers Corner building on Pequot Avenue in Oak Bluffs was dedicated as the 18th site on the African American Heritage Trail. A plaque was placed on the building honoring the role that is played in Island life by the Cottagers organization.

A group of never more than 100, the Cottagers are a group of professional African-American women who created their organization in 1956. Formed two years after Brown vs the Board of Education made segregation illegal in public schools and seven years before Dr. Martin Luther King shared his dream with the United States of America, this organization has worked tirelessly to promote education, a sense of cultural pride and the value of service to the community. Throughout the 1960s when American cities burned following the assassination of Dr. Martin Luther King, the women of the Cottagers continued their mission by providing summer activities for young people.

Their goal was, and still is, to contribute to the Vineyard community where many of their members' families have been seasonal residents for five generations. The Cottagers support the hospital, award a scholarship annually at the Regional High School, present an annual festival of African-American culture and have, for the past 50 years, empowered their members to play a significant role in the life of this Island community.

At the dedication of the Cottagers' building as a site on the Trail, Thelma Hurd, then president of the Cottagers organization, described the Cottagers as being "all about giving and restoring. We maintain what we have built and make plans for the future that will keep and honor the heritage of our past."

Noting that though her aunt had been a Cottager for 60 years she had not been able to become a member herself for several years as the rule of 100 members was strictly enforced. "I love the Vineyard and when I get here every year for July and August I can think of no greater pleasure than to sit on my deck and listen to the birds singing. This is a magical place, and we work hard to preserve this way of life that is so precious to us. We want to give back to a community that we value."

The Cottagers' building was packed for the dedication ceremony

Georgia Franklin

Jim Thomas

which began musically with a performance from the NAACP Spiritual Choir led by Jim Thomas. The choir gave an exuberant and passionate performance and the crucial importance of the spirituals as a form of coded communication for enslaved people was explained to the hushed audience. Significantly, Harry Burleigh who saved more than 3,000 spirituals by writing down their musical composition for posterity, was a frequent guest at the Shearer Cottage, the first site on the Heritage Trail. The presentation ended with a spirited rendition of "A Great Camp Meeting in the Promised Land."

The Cottagers' Corner building is an important site on the Trail honoring the hard work of these women and the role that they have played in the Island community. Over the years the building has been used for a variety of purposes including the After School Education Program and it is well known. The Heritage Trail organization recognized its cultural and educational significance. The women of the Cottagers are an important role model epitomizing the strength of women and of quiet, but determined, activism. As Thelma Hurd noted while accepting the award:

> *It is an honor to accept this plaque on behalf of a group of the smartest, most hard-working women that I have ever known. I am so proud of all of them and delighted that their work has been recognized as being worthy of being honored by dedicating our building as a site on the Trail.*

John F. Kennedy

"The heart of the question is whether all Americans are to be afforded equal rights and equal opportunities, whether we are going to treat our fellow Americans as we want to be treated. If an American, because his skin is dark, cannot eat lunch in a restaurant open to the public, if he cannot send his children to the best public school available, if he cannot vote for the public officials who represent him, if, in short, he cannot enjoy the full and free life which all of us want, then who among us would be content to have the color of his skin changed and stand in his place? Who among us would then be content with the counsels of patience and delay?"

—Televised address to the nation, June 1963

THE FOUNDATION OF THE
ISLAND CHAPTER OF THE NAACP

St. Andrews Episcopal Church,
Winter Street, Edgartown

1963
Dedicated 2007

In 1964 the MV branch of the NAACP was formed in response to the assassination of President John Kennedy. The founders were of all ethnicities and from all walks of life.

"Now I am proud of what we achieved, but back then I was just so angry."

– Audrey LeVasser
Founder member

Site 19 — Founding of Vineyard chapter NAACP

In June 1963, President Kennedy made a speech to the nation. His topic was the racial injustice that had prevented James Meredith from enrolling as a student at the University of Mississippi, but, unexpectedly, the president addressed racial issues not only in the south, but across the country. Quoting grim statistics on education, incarceration and economic freedom the president called on the nation to address the issues with honesty and clarity.

His message was heard on Martha's Vineyard where a

young Episcopalian minister, Henry Bird, was actively engaged in the civil rights movement. A ground swell of outrage was building on the Vineyard and a multi-ethnic group of people were discussing strategies. In November, the president was assassinated and on that very day the first, and still existent, chapter of the NAACP was formed on Martha's Vineyard. Its founding members included Audrey LeVasseur, Audria Tankard, Toby and Lucille Dorsey, Roscoe Heathman, George Jacobs, Virginia Mazer, Nancy Smith, Polly Murphy, Nancy Whiting, Peg Lillienthal and Kivi Kaplan. Kaplan is remembered as an incredibly effective recruiter for the organization and its most passionate advocate.

Speaking in 2010, Audrey LeVasseur commented: "Now I am proud of what we achieved, but back then I was just so angry all the time." For others too there was a sense of mission and obligation to their fellow human beings. Nancy Smith wrote eloquently to the *Vineyard Gazette* in defense of the Reverend Bird who was losing his Edgartown parish because of his civil rights advocacy.

St. Andrew's Episcopal Church, Edgartown

> *His protest in North Carolina removes another layer of my insulation against brotherhood, and melts some of my precious distinctions between Christians and non-Christians, Islanders and off-Islanders, good guys and bad guys.*

> *Before he acted I knew that I couldn't resign from the human race, or join a spiritual yacht club to avoid my connection with all people, but now*

I have to protest too. I have to declare war on the voices in my own heart that say, WAIT…. One person doesn't matter… what's the difference? Its not my fault. I expect the voices will keep right on yammering, but I won't believe them. I won't take them seriously any more.

Our treatment of Negro people in this country, on this Island, and off this Island has been, and is, unspeakably inhuman. Sometimes the inhumanity is obvious, sometimes subtle. I've really known this for a long time yet clung to the right to pretend….

Her letter concludes with a request for donations for the defense of Mr. Bird and his associates to be sent to Walter Stevenson, chairman of the NAACP's Falmouth chapter.

In a conversation in 2007, Reverend Bird reflected on his days in Edgartown and expressed surprise that St. Andrew's Episcopal church in the town was to be dedicated as a site on the African American Heritage Trail. His memories were not happy ones, but he was very happy to think that reconciliation had been achieved and to hear that the parishioners were delighted to be honored by the Heritage Trail.

In September 2007, St. Andrews Church was dedicated as the 20th site on the African American Heritage Trail honoring its history of civil rights activity and the fact that the first meeting of the Vineyard's NAACP chapter had been held there.

The dedication was very moving and the Rev. Bob Edmunds, the parish priest, spoke at length about reconciliation and advocacy against injustice. Alicia Knight's third grade students from Edgartown School attended as did several high school classes including two grandchildren of the founders: Michael Araujo, grandson of Audria Tankard and Toby Riseborough, grandson of Lucille and Toby Dorsey. Many members of St. Andrew's congregation attended and all joined hands to sing *We Shall Overcome* while Kate Taylor and Brian Scott performed songs from the spiritual tradition. One of the many roles of the African American Heritage Trail organization is to build and celebrate community, and this dedication was a wonderful example of that spirit.

A mobile exhibition of photographs of the founders has traveled throughout the Island and been exhibited in the schools and libraries.

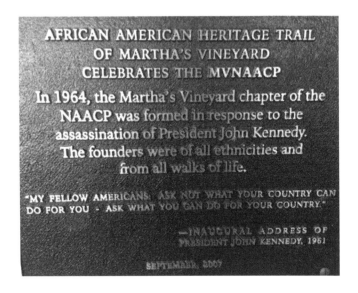

MEDGAR W EVERS

MISSISSIPPI

TEC 5
QMC

WORLD WAR II

JUL 2 1925
JUN 12 1963

Klu Klux Klan

Medgar Evers

Toby Dorsey, unknown,
George Jacobs, Kivie Kaplan

Myrlie Evers on the Vineyard

Sissie Tankard and Angela Waldron

Kivie Kaplan & Martin Luther King, Jr.

Edgartown 4th of July parade, 1964

THE VINEYARD FIVE

Former West Tisbury Library, Music Street, West Tisbury

1964

"I can't lock my doors because if you let a little fear in, pretty soon you're all fear."

—Sarah Small, 1964

In 1963 these five women traveled to North Carolina on a mission to register African-American voters. They organized and took action for justice.

Site #17 — The Vineyard Five

In 1964, five Vineyard women went to Williamston, North Carolina where the Reverend Bird had been involved in civil rights work. They were Virginia Mazer, Nancy Smith, Polly Murphy, Peg Lilienthal and Nancy Hodgson Whiting.

Inspired by a sense of mission and a desire to help in whatever way they could the women took 400 pounds of food and volunteered to assist in the struggle in North Carolina. Upon returning to the Vineyard following a stay in jail, Virginia Mazer told the *Vineyard Gazette*:

I think the most important thing about the trip

was what it did to us... our identification with the absolute degradation of human beings Once you have experienced that you have a new realization within yourself. You have shared the common lot and you realize that the club can fall on you.

Speaking in 2006, Nancy Hodgson Whiting reflected that the reason she had gone to North Carolina to join the struggle was that she did not want her children to look at her one day and ask why she did nothing in the greatest moral struggle of the century. "I was a divorced woman so I gave my mother a power of attorney and borrowed a coat. I went to the bank and put everything in order. My kids were teenagers, and I was afraid about what could happen."

Golden Frinks

To travel to the south the five women gave up their usual casual attire and dressed as "ladies" with hats and gloves. Their reasoning was that as white women dressed in that manner they would not be mistreated by the police in Williamston. That belief turned out to be false as all five were arrested, insulted and jailed.

The women had been asked by Golden Frinks, field secretary of the Southern Christian Leadership Conference, if they would take part in a demonstration. Things had been quiet for the previous month and Mr. Frinks saw the potential in these ladylike northerners publically protesting against segregation and injustice. He felt that their presence would be a morale booster for the African-American population just before voter registration was to begin. It was decided that the

Polly Murphy, Nancy Whiting, Peg Lilienthal, Virginia Mazer, Nancy Smith,

action would be at the Sears Roebuck store to protest their discriminatory hiring practices. Wearing their hats, gloves and Easter dresses, the five women armed with placards began their protest, and shortly afterwards the police arrived to arrest them.

Perhaps the most memorable exchange between them and the Williamston police was when Polly Murphy who was carrying a placard was accosted by a police officer who asked her did she know that she was breaking the law. "No" she replied "I thought I was granted that right under the Constitution." The officer replied "But this is Williamston and we have rules."

The women were booked and asked for identification whereupon Peg Lilienthal gave them her NAACP membership card. They were then ordered into cells where they saw the signatures of other civil rights protestors on the walls. The Reverend Bird's signature was there, and the women all signed their names in solidarity with him, and with the struggle. They were bailed out the following day by families back on the Vineyard and were driven to Freedom House the center of the Southern Christian Leadership Conference in Williamston.

While in Williamston, the women met Sarah Small who later visited the Vineyard bringing groups of African-American students to the Island. Holding her child whose name was spelled Freeda in a reference to the freedom struggle, Mrs. Small told them: "you are going so Freeda won't have to."

When the five women returned to the Vineyard, the relationship with Williamston continued and there were several visits and presentations from Sarah Small, Golden Frinks and groups of school children.

In 2007, the former library on Music Street in West Tisbury, where Nancy Hodgson Whiting was the librarian for many years, was the scene of a formal dedication of a plaque

Old West Tisbury Library

honoring these five women who risked so much in the struggle for justice. The families of the Vineyard Five were present as the plaque was unveiled, and the children of those brave women reflected on what had motivated their mothers to make that memorable trip.

Virginia Mazer's son Mark felt that his mother who had grown up in Mississippi as a Catholic and remembered the Klan burning a cross on the lawn of her school truly understood the nature of what was happening in the south. "I think she knew what the Klan was about and never forgot how frightened she was when they burned that cross."

"Hearing that she was going to the south was like kids today hearing that their mothers were going off to war in Iraq. I remember being so frightened for her" added Chris Murphy, son of Polly Murphy.

The consensus was that the Vineyard Five were determined to go because they were repelled by the brutal racism of the south, but they also realized that there was much to do to achieve justice in the north.

Welcome home, Vineyard Five!

THE POWER OF EDUCATION

First Educators of Color,
Spring Street, Vineyard Haven

1976-1992
Dedicated 2008

"Let us pick up our books and our pens" I said.
"They are the most powerful weapons. One child,
one teacher, one book and one pen can change the world."

—Malala Yousafzai

This plaque celebrates the achievements of African-American educators who forged a path for others to follow.

Site 21 — Vineyard Educators of Color

At dedication: Vera Shorter & Robert Tankard

The power of education to transform lives and to offer students access to the world is very apparent to the Heritage Trail organization, and while we advocate for inclusive classrooms and thoughtful, stimulating teaching materials we recognize the extraordinary value for all students of a multi-ethnic teaching staff and administration.

The core values of the organization are to promote community and celebrate diversity and in 2008 the Trail recognized the contributions made by those educators of color

152

AFRICAN AMERICAN HERITAGE TRAIL OF MARTHA'S VINEYARD

celebrates the achievements of

Rufus Shorter, superintendent of schools
1976-79
Robert Tankard, principal
1992-2001
Helen Vanderhoop Manning Murray, teacher and
member of the Wampanoag Tribe
1958-1984

African American educators who forged a path for others to follow.

"Our responsibility, as educators, is to respect and develop what is intrinsic
in our children so that they will learn to respect each other, and for this,
one earns the appreciation of all." Rufus Shorter

May 2008

who were the first to be appointed to positions within the school system. A plaque was placed on the superintendent's office on Spring Street in Vineyard Haven honoring three people who had played a significant role in lowering the barriers that had existed for people of color.

Helen Vanderhoop Manning Murray

Helen Vanderhoop Manning Murray who died on January 25, 2008 at the age of 89 had been the only teacher in the one-room school house in Aquinnah throughout the 1950s and '60s. A member of the Wampanoag Tribe who also celebrated

*Helen Vanderhoop
Manning Murray*

Rufus Shorter

her African-American heritage, Helen was a role model not only for the many students whom she taught but also for young women of color who were interested in becoming teachers.

I was lucky enough to have Helen Manning as my teacher and so I grew up with a sense of pride in being Indian and being a person of color. She gave that to me. (Adriana Ignacio 2008).

When the school in Aquinnah closed, Helen Manning became the special education teacher in Oak Bluffs from 1968 to 1984. Helen Manning Murray was passionately committed to education as means of advancement for the Wampanoag Tribe for whom she served as Tribal Education Director. Helen was the first teacher of color to serve in the Vineyard's school system.

Rufus Shorter

Rufus Shorter was the first African American superintendent of schools when he was appointed in 1976. He served until his death in 1980. He came to the Island following a career as a teacher and administrator in New York City. Though his tenure was short, Mr. Shorter was instrumental in building a major addition to the regional high school. The benefits of that addition included the expansion of the culinary arts and automotive trades departments, and the creation of the performing arts center. His work benefited the entire Island community. At the dedication of the site, Mr. Shorter's wife, Vera, recalled that her husband's passionate belief had been that every student could be successful and that inequities would be addressed through providing a superior education.

Robert Tankard

The third honoree was Robert Tankard who moved to the Vineyard from New Jersey when he was 16 and completed his education at the Regional High School on Martha's Vineyard. Mr. Tankard was a well-known football coach for many years and taught health and physical education at the Tisbury School. In 1993, he was appointed to the position of principal at the West Tisbury School following an acrimonious series of public meetings within the town. There were many who welcomed him to the position and many who vocally did not. The school committee eventually offered him the position and he remained at the school until his retirement in 2001.

Robert Tankard

> *It never hit me that I was the first black principal or that there would be any repercussions about that. The West Tisbury School Committee was very open and accepting.*

Mr. Tankard reflected in 2008: "We made it and we had a great run. It's a time I'll remember and cherish all my life." Since his retirement, Mr. Tankard has served as a school committee member for the town of Tisbury.

QUINTON M. BANNISTER

Martha's Vineyard Regional High School

1978-2010

"The time is always right to do what's right"

—Dr. Martin Luther King

First African-American teacher at MV Regional High School.

Site #22 — Quentin Bannister, MV Regional High School

In February 2010, the Heritage Trail organization honored another African-American educator by placing a plaque in the school recognizing the 32 years of service of Quinton Bannister, the first African-American teacher at the Regional High School.

Mr. Bannister moved to the Island from Washington DC when he was 16 and finished his high school education. Once he had completed college, he returned to the Vineyard and to the high school as a history teacher in the vocational program. In the summer seasons, he served as a police officer in the town of Tisbury. Later in his career, Mr. Bannister taught history and law and was known to all as QB.

Reflecting on the unique challenges faced by trail blazers, a high school senior Troy Small, who spoke at the dedication of the site, noted that there were unique and difficult challenges that faced anyone who challenged the status quo.

> *He's very well respected and highly regarded by everyone, but there have been times when it hasn't been easy (Troy Small, 2010).*

Thinking back on those times Mr. Bannister spoke of some of the hard days saying that he often looked to the posters in his room of Dr. Martin Luther King and Malcolm X saying "well, we got through another day my brothers."

There are two inscriptions on the plaque. The first: *we make the path by walking* is a reference to the civil rights struggle and the unsung heroes whose lives and careers serve as an inspiration.

The second is a quote from Dr. Martin Luther King Jr. *the time is always right to do what's right.* "I looked to him so often for inspiration" said Mr. Bannister.

Dorothy West

We have completed our plan to honor the former home of Dorothy West, novelist, storyteller and member of the Harlem Renaissance. Much has been written about Miss West whose works *The Wedding* and *The Living is Easy* are critically acclaimed. The Heritage Trail History Project is happy to honor her achievements, and acknowledge her many contributions to the life of this Island.

DOROTHY WEST –
Writer, Storyteller & Island Icon

Myrtle Avenue, the Highlands, Oak Bluffs

1907-1998
Dedicated: 2008

"There is no life that does not contribute to history"

—Dorothy West

T he former home of Dorothy West on Myrtle Avenue in Oak Bluffs was dedicated as a site on the Heritage Trail in August 2008. Ms. West who had spent summers on the Island as a child and later became well known as a member of the Harlem Renaissance had played a significant role in the life of Martha's Vineyard.

Harlem Renaissance writer and member of this community.

Site #13 — Dorothy West

In 1948, her book *The Living is Easy* was published. It is widely recognized as a work of literary significance whose characters are from a world of relative affluence and social mobility. Ms. West's work featured the world she knew well: the black bourgeoisie whose homes surrounded the Oval

Dorothy West

in Oak Bluffs where she made her home. Her most famous book *The Wedding* was not published until 1995 when it received great acclaim. Her editor at Doubleday publishers was Jacqueline Kennedy Onassis who was drawn to the work because of a common interest in Martha's Vineyard. Oprah filmed the story and Ms. West became internationally famous. Her 90th birthday was celebrated by the Town of Oak Bluffs. Hilary Clinton was a guest and a road in the Highlands was officially named Dorothy West Avenue.

Dorothy West had made her home on the Island for most of her adult life and she was well known within the community. She had worked in the hotel and restaurant trade, written a weekly column for many years for the *Vineyard Gazette* about life in Oak Bluffs and acted as a writing mentor for many high school English classes. She was a woman of very short stature and many remember how difficult it was to see her over the wheel of her large car. An annual scholarship is given in her memory each year at the Regional High School.

Speaking in the 1990s Ms. West recalled growing up in Oak Bluffs and how as a young girl she had often felt unwelcome at the town's pay beach. Her view of the racism of the time period was that it was often inspired by ignorance rather than malice.

> *I often felt that northern people did not know how to speak to black people, and southern people were much more comfortable interacting. I remember being on a bus and I said to the woman sitting next to me that I must get home*

and feed the birds and she replied that she did not know that black people fed the birds. That was it you see…. They didn't know. (conversation with Elaine Cawley Weintraub, 1990).

The dedication ceremony at Ms. West's former home was attended by a large crowd who shared their stories. Anne Peterson Jennings, a neighbor spoke: "I knew her as far back as when I was a young woman. She was just a wonderful neighbor, a beautiful person. I remember bringing my children to introduce to her. Everyone knew Dorothy West. She would have tea and everyone would chat and she loved children."

Lionel Bascom, a writer and admirer of Ms. West's work, traveled from Connecticut to attend the ceremony to pay tribute: "Dorothy is an icon on the Vineyard, yet she is also one of the 20th century's most accomplished story writers and she has never been given full credit for that."

AFRICAN AMERICAN HERITAGE TRAIL OF MARTHA'S VINEYARD celebrates the life and achievements of DOROTHY WEST, HARLEM RENAISSANCE WRITER AND MEMBER OF THIS COMMUNITY 1907-1998 "THERE IS NO LIFE THAT DOES NOT CONTRIBUTE TO HISTORY" DOROTHY WEST AUGUST 2008

Following the dedication ceremony, more than 50 guests traveled the Oak Bluffs section of the Heritage Trail returning to Shearer Cottage where Charles Ogletree spoke about the vitally important role of the Heritage Trail organization in preserving and celebrating African-American history.

Barber William H. Hammond

Some interesting information was uncovered by Island high school
teacher and historian Chris Baer. Using the census records of the
Vineyard, he investigated the life of Barber William H. Hammond. Born
in 1855 in Maryland, Mr. Hammond bought a property from the estate
of Sophronia P. Hancock of Tisbury. The building, on what is now Main
Street, Vineyard Haven, was used by Mr. Hammond as a barber shop.

Following the destruction of his premises by fire in 1883, the *Vineyard
Gazette* reported that he was getting ready to reestablish his business
at the old location. In December 1883, Mr. Hammond opened his
new barber shop. In July, 1899, a new boot-shining stand opened near
Hammond's barber shop. The 1900 census shows another African-
American barber living with Hammond, presumably working in his shop.
His name was John H. Foreman of North Carolina. William Hammond
married for the second time in 1906, and his premises are shown on the
Sanborn map of 1914 as a "barber shop." Many other barbers occupied
the property which was eventually known as Bert's Barber shop until the
most recent owner relocated to the Tisbury Market Place.

The board of the Heritage Trail History Project became very interested
in this story, and is pleased to have placed a plaque at the site of
Hammond's Barber shop to recognize his entrepreneurial and cultural
contribution of our Island. Such a dedication would be particularly
interesting because it would be the first dedication of a site in Tisbury.

BARBER HAMMOND

Main Street, Vineyard Haven

Early 20th century
Dedicated 2010

*"A man without ambition is dead. A man with ambition
but no love is dead. A man with ambition and love for
his blessings here on earth is ever so alive."*

—Pearl Bailey

*An African-American
entrepreneur who
bought property and
opened his barber
shop on Main Street in
Vineyard Haven.*

*Site #23 — Barber Hammond
Main Street, Vineyard Haven*

In February 2010, the African American Heritage Trail placed a plaque on the building on Main Street in Vineyard Haven that had once housed the barber's shop of Barber Hammond. Mr. Hammond who came to the Island with his wife whom he had married in New Bedford was the first, and only, African American to open a business in Vineyard Haven.

His first property was destroyed in the famous fire in Vineyard Haven in 1883, but he rebuilt and established a clientele within the town specializing in children's barbering needs. The barbershop was a new concept to the town, but it seems that Barber Hammond was extremely successful in establishing his business, and played an active role in the life of the town. He was a member of the town band as their drum major, and played on the baseball team.

William "Barber" Hammond

His wife, Ellen, was a steward on the steamship, and following her death it seems that Barber Hammond became involved in the life of Marion Lair, wife of local sea captain Leroy Lair. According to Chris Baer, a member of Mrs. Lair's family, Barber Hammond fathered a child, Ralph, with her, born on April 18, 1900.

Following the birth of this child it is believed that Marion Lair never left the house again presumably to "hide her shame" but her husband after several months' hesitation accepted Ralph as his son giving his name to him. In his piece

Vineyard Haven Main Street, c. 1900

1903 Champs!

in the *Dukes County Intelligencer*, "The Hole in the Bible," (Fall issue, 2009) Chris Baer described a literal hole in the Bible where his great-uncle Ralph was removed.

Inspired by his mother's desire to understand why her Uncle Ralph had disappeared from the family records, Chris Baer researched the story of both his great uncle, and the African-American man who was his father. The research strongly suggests that Barber Hammond, who was born in Maryland, was born into slavery, and his remarkable achievements in establishing a successful business are honored by the Heritage Trail.

Mr. Hammond's ambition and ability to function successfully within an almost all-white community are impressive and the path he and other determined individuals created have made this Island a more compassionate and inclusive environment.

AN AFRICAN AMERICAN ENTREPRENEUR WHO BOUGHT PROPERTY AND OPENED HIS BARBER SHOP IN 1880 ON THIS SITE

1974

THE TANKARD HOME

Glenwood Avenue, the Highlands, Oak Bluffs

1967-present
Dedicated 2012

"One's life has value as long as one attributes value to the lives of others by means of love, friendship, indignation and compassion."

—Simone de Beauvoir

The Tankard home in the Highlands area of Oak Bluffs was dedicated as a site on the Trail in 2012. This family have been actively involved in the local chapter of the NAACP since its earliest days and have been constant advocates for justice within the Island community.

Carrie and George Tankard moved to the Vineyard in 1967 fleeing from the riot-torn streets of Newark, New Jersey, and seeking a better life for their six children. The Vineyard was the destination of choice because George's mother, Audria, was living on the Island with several of his younger siblings.

This placque honors their contributions to the community of Martha's Vineuyard through their tireless advocacy for justice for all.

Site #24 — Tankard Home

It was a difficult time for Carrie who was used to urban living and was an active participant in her childrens' Parent Teacher Association, and other community organizations. "I didn't even know how to drive or how to live the country way. I had only ever lived in the city." (Carrie Camillo Tankard, 2012)

From the time of her arrival on the Vineyard, she became actively involved with the NAACP in a variety of roles ranging from advocacy, participating in selection committees for significant appointments, meeting with Island businesses and employers to advise on inclusive practices, liaison with the Island schools and celebration of cultural events. It was a lifetime commitment to the cause of justice for her and George.

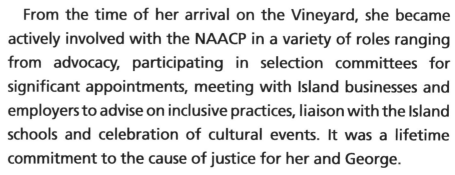

I always felt that it was very important not just to advocate for my own immediate family, but for everyone. Often I was a quiet warrior mostly because I hate speaking, but I was always there because the fight for inclusion and justice still needs attention. We have made progress, but

there is more to be made. (Carrie Camillo Tankard, 2012).

Until George's death in 2004, he was one of the tour guides for the Trail organization and did a wonderful job. At the time of his passing an appreciation of his work for the Trail was published by the *Boston Globe*. ("George Tankard brought history to tourists," Tom Long, July 29, 2004.)

George's quick wits, humor and ability to relate to everyone he met made him well known and loved in every part of the Island. Carrie has served for many years as vice president of the Vineyard's chapter of the NAACP and she is a member of the Cottagers organization. Together they devoted their lives to the service of their community. The Heritage Trail plaque outside their house on Glenwood Avenue bears the words from French philosopher Simone de Beauvoir: "One's life has value as long as one attributes value to the lives of others by means of love, friendship, indignation and compassion."

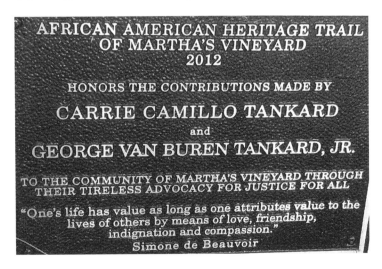

GRACE CHURCH,
Stained glass windows honoring
Absalom Jones & John Burgess

**Woodlawn Avenue at William Street
Vineyard Haven**

1804 & 1962

*Deep river, my home is over Jordan,
Deep river, Lord, I want to cross over into camp-ground.
Oh, don't you want to go to that gospel feast,
That promised land where all is peace?*

The Grace Episcopal Church in Vineyard Haven has two stained-glass windows that honor the first African-American Episcopal priest: Absalom Jones; and the first African-American Episcopal bishop: John Burgess.

Absalom Jones was born in Delaware into enslavement in 1746. Having taught himself to read primarily using the Bible, he became a lay minister and eventually bought his own

Two stained-glass windows honor the first Episcopal African-American priest and first Episcopal African-American bishop.

Site 20 — Grace Church

173

Reverend Absalom Jones
1746-1818

freedom in 1784. He served as lay minister for the black membership of St. George's Methodist Episcopal Church. An active evangelist, he greatly increased black membership at St. George's but when that church decided to segregate the black and white congregations he established the Free African Society to aid in the emancipation of enslaved Africans.

Absalom Jones established the first African church in Philadelphia and applied to join the Protestant Episcopal church. The following year the church was renamed the African Episcopal Church of St. Thomas and it was not until 1804 that Mr. Jones was ordained becoming the Episcopal Church's first African-American priest.

The Reverend John Melville Burgess, a resident of Vineyard Haven who worshipped at the Grace Church, was the Episcopal Church's first African American bishop. He was known for his lifelong inclusion of racial minorities, and his passionate advocacy for the poor. "I just wanted to prove that the Episcopal Church could be relevant to the lives of the poor," he reflected in a 1992 interview.

Born in Grand Rapids, Michigan, John Burgess devoted his life to the issues facing the poor and the under-represented in Michigan and then in Cincinnati. He understood the concerns of working people and the poor and provided effective leadership across lines of race and class.

In 1956, John Burgess moved to Massachusetts where in

1962 he was elected to the position of assisting bishop and in 1964 he was honored by *Time Magazine* as an

African-American who had broken barriers, earned a position of trust and become part of the leadership community in the US.

In 1969, the Episcopal Church elected him to the position of bishop making him the first African-American bishop in the Episcopal Church in the U.S.

In 1989, Bishop Burgess retired to Martha's Vineyard where he died in 2003.

Reverend John Burgess
1909-2003

COLEMAN'S CORNER

Myrtle Avenue, the Highlands, Oak Bluffs

1927
Dedicated: 2013

Ralf Coleman — Dean of Boston's Black Theatre, first black director of the WPA federal theater project

Granny Coleman — Her vision created Coleman corners in Oak Bluffs

"Spending summers here as children meant that no matter where we lived or traveled, coming back to the Vineyard, the Highlands… and especially to Coleman's Corners meant we were coming back … to a place… that our hearts call home."

—Jocelyn Coleman Walton

Site #25 — Coleman's Corner

The Coleman home was dedicated as site #25 on the Trail in July 2013. Five generations of the Coleman family have lived there since Luella Barnett Coleman came to work as a waitress on the Vineyard in 1927.

During the next few years she worked as a summer cleaner while boarding her children with friends in Vineyard Haven. In 1944, she saw the opportunity to become a property

Luella "Granny" Coleman

Luella & Rafe Coleman

owner in the Highlands and purchased her home from Manuel Gonsalves paying $800 for three lots.

In 1948, two more lots became available and Mr. Gonsalves wanted to give Mrs. Coleman the first option to buy, an opportunity that she took. Her family recall that she made a promise to Mr. Gonsalves that she would pay "a nickel down...and a nickel when you catch me." Her years of hard work made it possible for her to buy the property securing her family's continued presence on the Vineyard.

In 1956, she acquired three more lots on the opposite side of the road thus creating Coleman's Corners, a home for all of the extended family.

Luella Barnett Coleman's husband, Ralf Meshack Coleman was a presser in the Boston garment district, but his real and enduring passion was for the theater to which he devoted his life. He was an actor, a director, a producer and a playwright and his 50-year career helped shape Boston's Black Theater presence.

In 1934, he appeared on Broadway as the romantic lead in the black drama *Roll Sweet Chariot* and toured the US in a variety of roles. In 1935, he was appointed director of the Negro Federal Theater of Massachusetts, the first African-American director in FDR's WPA

Ralf Meshack Coleman

Federal Theater Project. For the next 40 years, he was active in black theater throughout Massachusetts and was very active in summer theater in Provincetown and Oak Bluffs.

In 1975, a year before his death, Boston's then Mayor, Kevin White, designated Ralf Coleman as the "Dean of Boston's Black Theater" and proclaimed October 5, 1975 as Boston's Ralf Coleman Day.

WPA Federal Theater Projec
New York Negro Unit: **MacBeth**

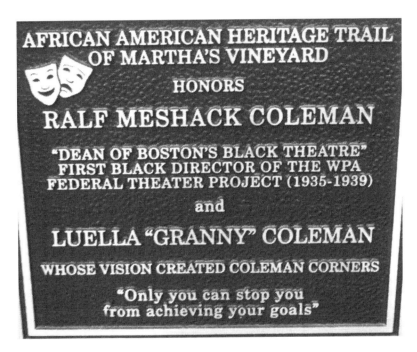

WPA Federal Theater Projec
New York Negro Unit: **MacBeth**

KNIGHTS OF PYTHIAS

cordially invites you to attend its

Monster **BOXING** *Benefit Show*

Under Auspices of Metropolitan A. A. U.

Presenting an Elaborate Program of

GOLDEN ★ GLOVES ★ BOUTS

National *and* State ★ Boxing Champions!

12—STAR AMATEUR BOUTS—12

Featuring a Special Boxing Exhibition between the
Internationally Famous Women Champions

EMMA MAITLAND (124 lbs.)

— vs. —

AURELIA WHEELDIN (118 lbs.)

and in addition, you will enjoy an

All Star Show of Broadway Entertainment!

Under the direction of Mike Hammer

Thursday, April 26, 1934

THIS THURSDAY EVENING at 8 o'clock P.M.

AT THE OLD LEVEL CLUB, 253 WEST 73rd STREET, NEW YORK

• DON'T MISS IT!

Tickets can be obtained at the Box Office

Choice Seats—$1.15 and $1.65—Includes Taxes

Proceeds for Our Relief Fund

EMMA CHAMBERS MAITLAND
World Female Lightweight Boxing Champion,

113 Dukes County Avenue, Oak Bluffs

1893-1975
Dedicated: 2015

"From now on, I'm to be what I'm to be"

—Emma Chambers Maitland

Emma Chambers Maitland was born Jane Chambers, in 1893 in Virginia. Her family were sharecroppers and descendents of enslaved people. She had seven brothers who to her own words "were rough country folk who had no way of improving themselves mentally, physically or financially."

At the age of ten while playing a game with her brothers she climbed a tree and fell from one of its branches suffering severe injuries that left her unable to move for several months.

"I can teach, sing, act, dance, box, wrestle or nurse. What would you prefer?" First licensed woman boxer in New York State, traveled through Europe, performed at the Moulin Rouge in Paris and in Shuffle Along and Black Birds in the U.S. She became a physical instructor and a nurse. "Stay young and enjoy good health" and "Clean living pays off."

Site 26 — Dukes County Avenue, Oak Bluffs

During this period of forced inactivity Jane spent much time pondering on her own future and comparing her ambitions to her brothers' lack of ambition.

During this time, a priest from the local convent visited and suggested that Jane go to the convent to be educated. Her father was apparently very suspicious of that idea feeling that Jane was "stuck up and trying to act like white folk. You have to get into the field and hoe corn like the others around" (Emma Chambers Maitland's recollections). She managed to spend three years at the convent and gained an education but had to return to the farm when her mother became sick.

Her next ambition was to take the test that would qualify her as a teacher in the local schools for children of color. Again she was faced with family opposition, but she managed to recruit allies at the convent to help her and she took the test, passing it. Her family warned her that her father was very angry and intended to make her leave the farm to which, Jane responded

> *I certainly can go because I went away and took the examination, and I am going to be one of these first class school teachers. I am through killing tobacco worms...(Emma Chambers Maitland's recollections).*

Jane was appointed to a school and began her career. She was frustrated by what she saw as the students' lack of interest but was particularly concerned about a boy whose life was extremely difficult and she spent time mentoring him and working hard to give him an opportunity.

In her own words, after two years she was bored and wanted to move on, and at that point she did move to Washington DC where she met her husband-to-be, Clarence Maitland, who was completing his medical studies at Howard University. They married and Emma gave birth to a daughter. Within one year of their marriage, Clarence died of tuberculosis leaving Emma alone with a baby. "Within one year, I was a fiancée, a wife, a mother and a widow."

Alone in the world with a child to care for, Emma decided to seek her fortune as a dancer and an actress. With the same strength of character that had enabled her to pass the teachers' test, Emma left her child with her parents and headed to Paris where she danced in cabaret and even at the famous Moulin Rouge.

She traveled throughout Europe as a dancer and, according to family stories, at one of her dancing engagements she had to strenuously rebuff the advances of an Irish aristocrat at whose home she was dancing. It must have been difficult in the early years of the 20th century for a dancer not to be viewed as a woman who would welcome such advances. Perhaps as a result of that experience, Emma, as she was now known, began to train with the heavyweight boxing champion, Jack Taylor, and returned to the U.S. as a certified boxer.

In 1927, she appeared in a boxing skit during her dance

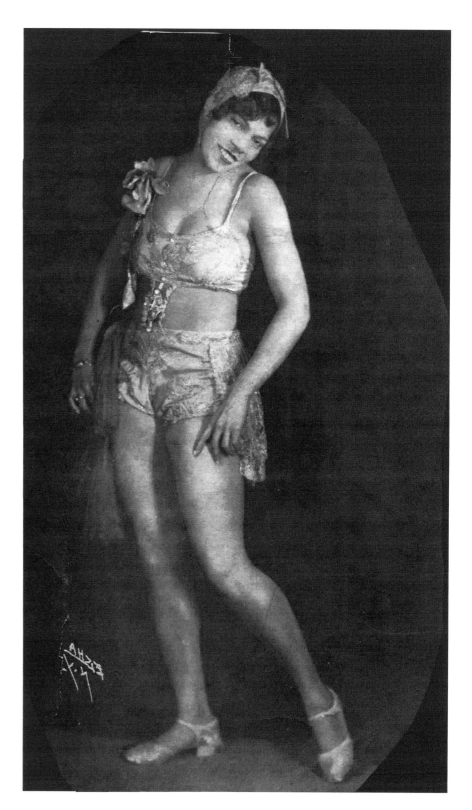

performance in Paris. She and fellow American, Aurelia Wheeldin, boxed for three rounds during their stage act. Both women had filed for licenses to box the French female boxing champion, Jeanne Le Mar. The spring 2013 edition of the *Journal of Sport* featured a photograph of Emma Chambers Maitland and Aurelia Wheeldin boxing in Paris in their *Tea for Two* revue. Emma was extremely successful and earned $500 a fight and was recognized as the world female champion. The photographs taken of her during her boxing career show that dancing in exotic costumes were part of her performances.

When she returned to the U.S. Emma was very involved in the Harlem Renaissance movement. She appeared in the musical *Shuffle Along*, the first Broadway musical written,

produced and performed by African Americans. In 1929, she appeared in the theater production of *Harlem* by Wallace Thurman and William Rapp, at the Apollo Theater.

Emma's nephew, Frank Chambers, recalls that his Aunt Maitland was a strong believer in womens' rights and at one point in her career she worked as bodyguard for a woman who had inherited a considerable fortune in stocks. As women were not then allowed to hold the floor on the stock exchange she hired Emma to protect her if anyone tried to eject her when she entered the building.

He recalls that when Emma retired from boxing she still used to wrestle and eventually taught dance and gymnastics in New York City. She had a strong dislike for smoking and was an advocate of living a healthy life style. During this time period, Emma bought a home on Dukes County Avenue in Oak Bluffs where she spent the summers and eventually it became her retirement home.

She is fondly remembered by Jacqueline Hunt, former president of the local NAACP chapter, who recalls her as "wearing braids when no one was wearing braids."

Emma apparently intervened on the beach when some boys were teasing Jacqueline and ducking her in the water. Emma told her she needed to learn to swim, and then she taught her how to. That story expresses very clearly Emma's rule for life. She did not believe that there was a problem that one could not solve, but she knew the value of self reliance.

Emma had begun her life's work as a tobacco farmer, then a school teacher, a traveling dancer, a stage performer, a boxer and a teacher of gymnastics, but she had one more career that she wanted to add. In her latter years, she qualified as a nurse. She died in 1975 at the age of 82, and her remarkable story had all but disappeared.

Thanks to the generosity of her nephew, Frank Chambers, I have become aware of Emma's story. She embodies all that our organization values. She is an incredible role model for young women who wonder about their own possibilities and for all people everywhere. Her life is the story of a woman who never accepted the limitations placed on her. She was a fighter in every sense of the word, from her earliest days working in the tobacco fields through her years of international travel and theatrical revue and her success as world boxing champion. She embraced life with both hands seeing potential in every situation.

In an age when for a young woman of color born into poverty the possibilities were very limited, she broke all the rules and her courage and talents deserve to be remembered. The Heritage Trail is proud to celebrate her life.

Harlem Renaissance

The Harlem Renaissance, a period of intense creativity named after its cultural center, Harlem, New York, spanned the period from the end of World War I until the 1930s. This flowering of African-American talent broke barriers in terms of music, literature, poetry and art and brought African-American culture onto the world's stage. The writers James Weldon Johnson, Langston Hughes, Countee Cullen, Zora Neale Hurston brought to the world a picture of African-American life. Intellectuals such as W. E.B. Du Bois, activists such as A. Phillip Randolph, singers such as Paul Robeon and the famous dancer Josephine Baker acted as the ambassadors of a vital and vibrant culture. This was the era when the great jazz musicians were literally changing the world and dominating the national culture. African-American music and dance was a huge attraction in France and many dancers like Josephine Baker and Emma Chambers Maitland performed there. Martha's Vineyard became home to many of those artists who were part of this vibrant

Paul Robeson

culture. Paul Robeson was a regular visitor at the Shearer Cottage; and Elizabeth White, granddaughter of Charles Shearer, created entirely African-American presentations of *Othello* at her home in Oak Bluffs. Harry Burleigh, who sang for the King of England, saved more than 3,000 spirituals by writing them musically so that they would no longer be preserved only through the oral tradition. He was a guest of many years standing at the Shearer Cottage.

Ralf Coleman, the Dean of Boston's Black Theater and whose home is a site on the Trail, presented black theater in Boston, and throughout the country. Dorothy West, often referred to ask "the kid," was a member the Harlem Renaissance and worked with those famous writers. Belle Powell danced in the first presentation of the stage show *Harlem*. The Renaissance flowered here on the Vineyard where the culture of creativity thrived. Nobody embodies those exciting times more than Emma Chambers Maitland who danced in Paris and New York and appeared in the first fully African-American theater performances *Shuffle Along* and *Harlem*.

Martha's Vineyard was a safe and welcoming place where these talented individuals were able to fulfill their creative ambitions and celebrate African-American culture.

I, Too

I, too, sing America.

I am the darker brother.
They send me to eat in the kitchen
When company comes,
But I laugh,
And eat well,
And grow strong.

Tomorrow,
I'll be at the table
When company comes.
Nobody'll dare
Say to me,
"Eat in the kitchen,"
Then.

Besides,
They'll see how beautiful I am
And be ashamed—

I, too, am America.

Langston Hughes,
1902-1967

Sites on African-American Heritage Trail of Martha's Vineyard

History is the story of the struggles, joys & cultural values that give meaning to all our lives. It is the human story.

Site #1: Rebecca Amos, the woman from Africa, Great Bight Reserve, North Road, Chilmark.

Site #2: Randall Burton, the escape from enslavement. One plaque on tribal land at West Basin Aquinnah, and one at Menemsha.

Site #3: Nancy Michael, wise woman. Memorial Wharf, Edgartown.

Site #4: Captain William Martin, African-American Whaling Captain, Chappaquiddick Island.

Site #5: Gravesite of William Martin and Sarah Brown, Chappaquiddick Cemetery.

Site #6: Pulpit Rock dedicated to John Saunders, Methodist exhorter. Land Bank property off Pulpit Rock Way, off County Road, Oak Bluffs.

Site #7: Miss Louisa Izett, entrepreneur, 121 South Circuit Avenue, Oak Bluffs.

Site #8: The Landladies of Oak Bluffs, bench in Hiawatha Park, South Circuit Avenue, Oak Bluffs.

Site #9: Old Marine Cemetery, Lobster Hatchery, Shirley Avenue, Oak Bluffs. Dedicated to the life of Rebecca Martin.

The founders of the Trail, Elaine Cawley Weintraub and Carrie Camillo Tankard share the Trail with Congressman Gregory Meeks of Queens, New York and Congresswoman Barbara Lee of Oakland, California in 2014. From left: Congressman Meeks, Elaine Cawley Weintraub, Carrie Camillo Tankard and Congresswoman Lee.

Site #10: Shearer Cottage, Rose Avenue, Highlands, Oak Bluffs. The oldest African-American owned guesthouse on the Vineyard. Still owned and operated by the family of Charles and Henrietta Shearer.

Site #11: Bradley Memorial church, Masonic Avenue, Oak Bluffs.

Site #12: The Powell House. The former home of Adam Clayton Powell and Isabel Washington Powell, Dorothy West Avenue, Highlands, Oak Bluffs.

Site #13: The former home of Dorothy West, famed Harlem Renaissance writer, Myrtle Avenue, Highlands, Oak Bluffs.

Site #14: The former home of Senator Edward Brooke, US Senator and Massachusetts Attorney General, Nashawena Park, Oak Bluffs.

Site #15: The former home of the Overton family (the summer White House of the Civil Rights Movement), Corner of Narragansett Avenue and Seaview Avenue, Oak Bluffs.

Site #16: Basketball teams of the 1970s at the Martha's Vineyard Regional High School, Edgartown Road, Oak Bluffs.

Site #17: The Vineyard Five, Civil Rights activists, the old library, Music Street, West Tisbury.

Site #18: The Cottagers' organization, a group of 100 African-American women dedicated to serving their Island community, 57 Pequot Avenue, Oak Bluffs.

Site #19: The MV NAACP chapter founded in 1963, St. Andrews Church, 51 Winter Street, Edgartown.

Site #20: Grace Church, stained glass window honoring Absalom Jones, the first African-American Episcopal priest and John Burgess, the first African-American Episcopal bishop, Woodlawn Avenue, Vineyard Haven.

Site #21: Education Pioneers, the first African-American people working within the school system, office of the school superintendent, Spring Street, Vineyard Haven.

Site #22: Quinton Bannister, the first African-American teacher at Martha's Vineyard Regional High School, Edgartown Road, Oak Bluffs.

Site #23: Barber Hammond, first African-American entrepreneur, Main Street, Vineyard Haven.

Site #24: The Tankard home, community activists Carrie and George Tankard, Glenwood Avenue, Highlands, Oak Bluffs.

Site #25: Coleman's Corners, Ralf Coleman and Louella Coleman, black theater, Dorothy West Avenue, Highlands, Oak Bluffs.

Site #26: Former home of Emma Chambers Maitland, world female boxing champion, dancer, educator and nurse. Dukes County Avenue, Oak Bluffs.

ILLUSTRATIONS

Cover page photograph of Jaquelle Servance as Rebecca Amos by Charlie Utz.

Opening photographs from Jannifer, Overton and Maitland family collections, the Shearer Cottage and website.

Sale of slave boy document from Martha's Martha's Vineyard Museum.

Photograph of George Tankard by Tony Bowyer.

Photographs of Pulpit Rock, Old Marine Cemetery and Martin House by Craig McCormack.

Photograph of Serel Garvin unveiling the Heritage Trail plaque in Aquinnah with Elaine Cawley Weintraub, taken by Robert C. Hayden.

Photograph of the Menemsha School third grade class visiting the Heritage Trail plaque in Aquinnah by Elaine Cawley Weintraub.

Photograph of William Vanderhoop (seated) and Woody Vanderhoop, Jason Baird and David Vanderhoop of the Wampanoag Tribe drumming at the Heritage Trail dedication in Aquinnah taken by Joseph C. Carter.

Photographs of *Amistad* courtesy of Sail Martha's Vineyard.

Photograph of Jaquelle Servance as Rebecca Amos by Charlie Utz.

Photograph of Rebecca's field by Carrie Camillo Tankard.

196

Photograph of Dana Carberry as Nancy Michael by Craig McCormack.

Photograph of Heritage Trail plaque to Rebecca Michael at the Old Marine Cemetery by Mark Alan Lovewell.

Portrait of William A. Martin by John Belain.

Photograph of log book cover from *Europa* by Elaine Cawley Weintraub.

Photograph of William and Sarah Martin's grave on Chappaquiddick by Elaine Cawley Weintraub.

Photograph of the Shearer Cottage by Craig McCormack.

Photograph of the Shearer Cottage Heritage Trail plaque by Mark Alan Lovewell.

Photograph of Rev. Denniston and the Bradley Memorial Chapel from the Martha's Vineyard Museum.

Photograph of African American soldiers with French regiment during WW 1 from the Jannifer collection.

Photographs of Louisa Izett and Georgia O'Brien by Tony Bowyer.

Photograph of Ora McFarlane and Lillian Garcia by Tony Bowyer.

Photograph of the Powell house by Craig McCormack.

Photograph of the Powell house Heritage Trail plaque by Mark Alan Lovewell.

Photograph of the Overton house by Mark Alan Lovewell.

Photographic portrait of Joseph Overton and photograph of Joseph Overton with Fidel Castro at the Hotel Theresa in Harlem, New York, from the Overton family collection.

Photograph of the Heritage Trail plaque at the former home of Senator Edward Brooke by Mark Alan Lovewell.

Photographs of the murals at the Martha's Vineyard Regional High School all photographs by Mark Alan Lovewell.

Nancy Michael mural by Joe Murphy.

William A. Martin mural by Bronwyn Burns.

Heritage Trail map mural by Brooke Emin and Lauraye White.

Rebecca Amos with Nancy Michael mural by Elyse Fortes and Lily Morris.

Photograph of Jade Cash, Jarrett Campbell & Brian Scott with Elaine Cawley Weintraub by Carrie Camillo Tankard.

Photograph of former African American church on Dukes County Avenue, Oak Bluffs by Carrie Camillo Tankard.

Photograph of Barber Hammond courtesy of Chris Baer.

Photograph of Vineyard Five courtesy Martha's Vineyard Museum.

Photographs of Emma Chambers Maitland courtesy of Frank Chambers.

Additional 2nd edition photogaphs from the Heritage Trail website and internet.

BIBLIOGRAPHY

Aaronowitz D. & Giroux H., (1991) *Post-Modern Education: Politics, Culture & Social Criticism,* Minneapolis, University of Minnesota.

Bolster, Jeffrey, (1997) *Black Jacks, African Americans in the Age of Sail,* Harvard University Press.

The Dukes County Intelligencer, Martha's Vineyard Museum

"The Diaries of Jeremiah Pease," ed. Arthur Railton, 1983

"The History of Oak Bluffs, by Adelaide Cromwell, 1984

"The African American Presence on Martha's Vineyard," by Jaqueline Holland, August 1991

"When Jail Was a Gaol, Not a House of Correction," by Arthur Railton, 1998

"Sharper Michael Born a Slave — First Islander Killed in the Revolution," by R. Andrew Pierce, May 2005

Dukes County Registry of Probate — Will of William A. Martin

Greene, Lorenzo Johnston, (1974) *The Negro in Colonial New England,* Athenaeum, New York.

Hayden, Robert C. and Karen E. (1999) *African Americans on Martha's Vineyard and Nantucket,* Select Publications.

Hegerty, R. B. (1959) *Returns of the Whaling Vessels Sailing from American Ports — A Continuation of Alexander Starbuck's History of the American Whale Fishery 1896-1928,* New Bedford, Old Dartmouth Historical Society.

Higginbotham, A. Leon, Jr. (1978) *In the Matter of Color,* Oxford University Press.

Horton, James O. and Lois E., (2001) *Hard Road to Freedom, the Story of African America,* Rutgers University Press.

Milton, John Earle, (1861) *Report to the Governor and Council of the Commonwealth of Massachusetts on the condition of the Indians of Chappaquiddick and Martha's Vineyard,* Widener Library at Harvard University.

Molloy, Mary, (1990) *African Americans in the Maritime Trades: A Guide to Resources in New England,* Kendall Whaling Museum Monograph Series No.6, Kendall Whaling Museum, Sharon, Massachusetts.

Sewall, S. (1968), The Selling of Joseph (an essay first published in 1700). In G. Moore Notes on slavery in Massachusetts (pp. 83-87), New York, Negro University Press.

Sloan S., Stirling C. et al, (2002) *Main Streets and Back Roads of New England,* Globe Pequot Press, 2002

Spring, J. (1997), *Deculturalization and the Struggle for Equality,* New York, McGraw-Hill.

Weintraub, Elaine Cawley, (1993) "The African American History of Martha's Vineyard," *New England Journal of History,* Fall.

Weintraub, Elaine Cawley, (2000) *Lost Histories & Lost Heroes: The African American Heritage Trail of Martha's Vineyard,* Organization of American Historians.

Weintraub, Elaine Cawley, (2005) *Where Were All the Black People Then? The African American Heritage Trail of Martha's Vineyard,* Mystic Seaport Museum.